D1499234

Philosophical Foundations
of the Curriculum

RAND McNALLY CURRICULUM SERIES

EDITED BY J. CECIL PARKER,
UNIVERSITY OF CALIFORNIA

Philosophical Foundations

of the Curriculum

BY

Tom C. Venable,
INDIANA STATE UNIVERSITY

RAND McNALLY & COMPANY • CHICAGO

Rand McNally Education Series
B. Othanel Smith, Advisory Editor

Rand McNally Curriculum Series, edited by J. Cecil Parker

Ford and Pugno, eds., *The Structure of Knowledge and the Curriculum*
Parker and Rubin, *Process as Content*
Venable, *Philosophical Foundations of the Curriculum*
Wellington and Wellington, *The Underachiever: Challenges and Guidelines*

Also published by Rand McNally:

Gage, ed., *Handbook of Research on Teaching*—A Project of the American Educational Research Association

PREFACE

●

No author can possibly give credit to all who helped him produce his manuscript, for all of the people who have contributed to his experiences have aided in making his work come to life. There are, however, several people whose contributions have been particularly helpful to me in this effort.

Two Englishmen provided the major inspiration for this text. The first was Winston Churchill, whose statement, "Short words are best and old words when short are the best of all," has been a guideline in all of my teaching and writing. The second was W. A. Sinclair, whose little book, *Introduction to Philosophy*, epitomizes Churchill's assertion. When the idea of the present volume occurred to me, I determined to follow the advice of Churchill and the model of Sinclair. It has not been an easy task. Such writing is most difficult, and critics and editors continually accuse one of oversimplification. If error must exist, I would prefer that it be in that direction. The reader must determine for himself whether I have accomplished my ideal.

Among those who helped more directly, special appreciation is expressed to students in my classes who criticized this material in lecture form; to Alan Johnson, who uncovered some information which was of tremendous aid; and to Carol Rumbaugh, who typed the manuscript.

The manuscript would not have been possible without the proofreading of my wife, Helen; the critical evaluation of Dr. Mary Ann Carroll; and the suggestions of one of Rand McNally's editors whose identity I do not know.

Tom C. Venable

Terre Haute, Indiana
November, 1966

CONTENTS

•

CONTENTS

•

CHAPTER I

PHILOSOPHY AND THE CURRICULUM

"It's good theory but it won't work." How often we hear this statement concerning our educational ideas and pronouncements. Principles expounded by educational theorists often seem far removed from the classroom teacher faced with a roomful of energetic kids he must control, care for, and teach. Yet this frequently voiced criticism contains an inconsistency. For if theory is good, it will work; and if it will not work, it is not good theory.

Why, then, do teachers cry out against theory? Do we actually distrust it? Do we really find it unusable? Or is it possible that the fault lies not within the theory but within ourselves? Is it not possible that each of us is so pressed by the here-and-now of our educational tasks that we do not take the time to question, examine, and recreate the theory back of our practices? Such examination might well prove that we have not developed consistent, meaningful theories to guide our teaching.

We are inclined to make statements about our beliefs which are in conflict with each other and with our actual practices. A prominent television personality may be an avid supporter of the mental health movement but at the same time criticize the idea of teachers' being concerned with the emotional adjustment of students. A teacher may extoll the glories of the democratic way of life and yet become the absolute dictator of all that occurs in his classroom. Consistency between beliefs and the development of practices growing out of these beliefs are all too rare among those of us who are concerned with education.

Lacking this consistency, we may find ourselves giving lip service to two or more conflicting views, or professing one belief while our behavior evidences another, or—worst of all—allowing our behavior to be determined by forces that bear no relationship to any particular set of principles.

THE BASES OF CURRICULUM CHOICES

If belief does not determine behavior, what does? When we decide to include certain subjects in our curriculum and omit others, what makes us do so? There are several possible answers to such a question. Let us examine a few.

Much of our behavior—particularly our classroom practice—is the result of what we have known others to do. We feel a safety in numbers. The fact that other teachers select specific content or use certain techniques in teaching may cause us to fall in line with them. Why should the literature instructor teach *Macbeth* only during the senior year of high school? The answer is probably that "everyone else does." A teacher who varies from this pattern may be regarded with suspicion by his colleagues. It is easy to drift along with the majority and to adopt the attitude that "fifty million Frenchmen can't be wrong." To many this is reason enough to teach as they do.

But such a reason for behavior may be the cause of grave errors. If the majority is wrong—and wrong it can be—we can make difficulties for ourselves by moving with the stream, no matter how large the majority may be. There is little comfort to the victim of a shipwreck in knowing that the rest of the crew is going down with him. There was a time when the majority thought the earth to be flat, diseases to be caused by demons, and the fate of man to be governed by the stars. But such beliefs and the practices which grew out of them contributed nothing to the well-being of either the individual or the society.

The type of curriculum we develop may also be the result of our imitation of other programs of instruction. If certain schools achieve wide publicity for the development of certain curriculum practices, we may, in turn, attempt to install a similar program in our own schools. Certainly we learn a great deal by the sharing of experiences, but such imitation is valuable only if the model we choose reflects a point of view or principles which are sound. A program may be effective in one situation, but in other situations and with other groups prove inadequate.

Many undesirable curriculum practices have been perpetuated because at one time they were reported successful and have since been imitated and emulated by others without ever being questioned or evaluated in the light of more critical examination.

Often our behavior is governed by no factor other than our emotional acceptance of the behavior. If it "feels good" for us to engage in some activity, we are likely to repeat the act; and if it doesn't give emotional satisfaction, we are likely to discontinue it. For example, a teacher may administer—or refrain from administering—physical punishment merely because of his emotional reaction to such practices. We are all likely to resemble the English teacher who taught her students about the process of engraving formal announcements and who, when asked why, replied, "I know it has nothing to do with English, but I do love to talk about it."

To use emotional satisfaction as the sole guideline for curriculum development is to open a Pandora's box of vague goals and lack of order and system. Emotional reactions can be deceptive and disorderly. Freudian psychology makes us aware of the depth and the complexities from which these emotional reactions may arise. To have no emotional reactions would make for a dull life indeed, but for the curriculum to be determined by this criterion alone would provide an educational system which could only be chaotic.

Finally, behavior may be determined by what seems to work. The teacher who presents subject matter in a certain way and finds his pupils learn more than if he uses some other method tends to repeat his success. An instructor may use time lines to aid his students in understanding the sequence of historical events. If the practice proves successful, he will continue to use the technique and may even enlarge upon it, using similar devices elsewhere in his teaching.

Although each of us is likely to have his behavior influenced greatly by his past successes, there is in such practice the danger that he will gain success in one area only to suffer failure in another. To motivate the child to learn by using threat of punishment may cause him to be a better learner, but it may also cause him anxieties and tensions which will plague him the rest of his life. The English teacher who disciplines his class by having his troublemakers memorize poetry may have well-be-haved pupils, but he can be asked, "Isn't your aim to get students to like poetry? Then how will they learn to like what they associate with punishment?"

The four factors suggested in the preceding paragraphs are all important in determining how we will behave in various day-to-day situations. However, each has its fallacies and pitfalls. The need for avoiding these errors is particularly vital for the teacher inasmuch as his students are the most valuable of resources. How can this be done? How can the curriculum be organized and developed so as to assure our maximum success? Are there other guidelines for curriculum development which may be less dangerous and more rewarding? In short, can we find better alternatives? Let us investigate.

ASSUMPTIONS AND BEHAVIOR

All of our behavior ultimately rests on certain assumptions—assumptions we make about the world and our place in it. The man who worships in his church makes certain assumptions about his God and his relationship to Him; the doctor who strives to save his patient's life assumes that the life is worth saving; the housewife who works for the comfort and well-being of the members of her family makes assumptions about their relationship to her and to each other; even the scientist who is concerned only with the materials of his experiment assumes that his experience is real and not just a dream.

The assumptions we make are many and varied. Some we are fully conscious of making; others, however, we make without awareness; it is not until we are called upon to explain our behavior that we realize that such assumptions exist. How many times we find ourselves saying, "But I thought . . ." or, "I had assumed that . . . !"

If the assumptions we make are good assumptions—that is, if they are *sound*—our resulting behavior will be profitable. But if we base our behavior on assumptions which are not sound, the resulting behavior is almost certain to prove unrewarding or frustrating. Let us imagine, for instance, a teacher who distrusts his students. There *are* teachers who believe that the pupils are continually attempting to escape from their learning tasks, to cheat, and to make the teacher's task unpleasant and unrewarding. Such an assumption could lead to the teacher's warning, threatening, and policing the students. They might respond by living up to his expectations of them. But whether they do or not, his suspicions and distrusts are certain to lead him to a state where his teaching will become onerous and frustrating. Here, the unsound assumption that the teacher has made has led to behavior which is unprofitable and frustrating.

But a logical question can come from this: *How do we know if our assumptions are sound?* It is one thing to say that our assumptions should be sound; it is quite another to determine if they are. We have illustrated the importance of relating our behavior to our assumptions only to reveal a greater problem.

ENTER THE PHILOSOPHER

It is at this point that the philosopher can come to our aid. One way in which we may view the role or task of the philosopher is that he aids us in the examination of our assumptions. Each of us, as he continually tests his beliefs and concepts in the light of logic and of their consequences, is engaged in the study of philosophy. To the extent that we are willing to lay bare our assumptions, dissect them, study them, and discard or reaccept them, to that extent, each of us is a philosopher.

Let us return to an earlier question, "Is there another way to develop guides to curriculum practices which are better than those which we traditionally rely on?" Our answer is "Yes," and it is the way of philosophy. For each of us has within him the power to become an examiner of assumptions. It is hard work, but it is through the study of philosophy that we can come to the best decisions about the soundness of our behavior.

To the person engaged in teaching such a quest is particularly rewarding. For the task of the teacher demands a particular kind of dedication. The teacher who does not perform at the highest level of his potentialities is guilty of an unforgivable neglect. The shaping of behavior in terms of sound assumptions is one of the best ways to make the teacher an effective agent in the learning process.

The study of philosophy is not like the study of any other

subject. One can study *about* philosophy in the same way one studies other subjects such as history or economics; but the study *of* philosophy requires the individual to take on new ways of thinking. It requires the student to actively engage in the examination of his own assumptions. In this respect no one can teach philosophy; no book can make one think philosophically. The best a teacher or author can do is to lead the student's thinking, to serve as a guide on his journey through the wilderness of his own thoughts. The study of philosophy is not a study of new facts, although on occasion one may discover such new material; it is, rather, the examination of old and familiar material in a new way. It demands, therefore, that the student divorce himself from his traditional view of himself and his world and that he leave behind his prejudices and preconceived ideas. This is not easy, and few of us are ever completely successful in doing it. Nevertheless, if the student is willing to do so, the study of philosophy can be one of life's most rewarding adventures.

How does the philosopher go about his work? How do we question our assumptions? We may be willing to engage in such an adventure in ideas, but how do we proceed? An assumption is defined as something which is taken for granted or supposed and, therefore, cannot be verified in a scientific sense. If an idea can be proved, it ceases to be an assumption and becomes a fact. It is these unproved and unprovable ideas on which we must fix our attention. At the risk of oversimplification, let us set down some principles or criteria by which our assumptions may be examined and evaluated.

First, we can examine our assumptions in light of their reliability. That is, we may ask the question, "Can we depend on the belief to always result in the same outcome?" It is possible for us to hold a view which may be illogical when applied to the realities of living. We may, in other words, accept certain convictions which have little to do with the problems we must face.

Anthropologists tell us of certain primitive peoples who perform a ritual each year for the coming of spring. These natives do not see the rites as a tribute or celebration of the change of season; they believe their efforts *cause* the budding of trees, the greening of the fields, and the arrival of spring showers. But should these primitive peoples fail to complete their ritual, spring would still come! Their assumption lacks reliability. However, before we smile with sophistication at their naiveté, let us ask ourselves if each of us does not have assumptions about his own manner of life that have never been put to any logical or practical test of reliability. It is not uncommon for us to hold tenaciously to some assumption long after its reliability has been disproved or its usefulness has ceased to exist.

Second, we may examine the validity of our assumptions. By validity is meant whether our beliefs conform to our new knowledge and experiences. Our knowledge of the universe and of ourselves is continually expanding. As new discoveries are made, they may be used to test our previously held concepts. When this occurs, we must either reexamine our assumptions in light of the new facts or we must deny the existence of the discovery. If we accept the latter course, we may burn our scientists at the stake; but their discoveries will continue to haunt us, for our false assumptions have led us to behavior which no longer meets the challenge of changing conditions. Since Darwin expounded his evolutionary theories more than a century ago, he and his followers have been maligned by many well-meaning people whose beliefs could not tolerate the presence of Darwin's views. Rather than examining their own assumptions, these people attacked what Darwin had written—often without taking the trouble to read *The Origin of Species*. Had their own assumptions been valid, these men could have accepted the views of Darwin and still held to their own beliefs. But their assumptions fell before the criterion of validity; and as a result, they rejected the discoveries of the biologist.

A final criterion is that of consistency. Inasmuch as assumptions are nonprovable, it is important that the beliefs support—rather than work against—each other. As an example, mathematicians have created several different systems of geometry. Euclidian geometry starts with a certain set of postulates and builds its system of theorems on these postulates; non-Euclidian geometry begins with different sets of postulates and likewise builds *its* system. Neither system may be proved to be more accurate or more valid than the other, but each has internal consistency.

Likewise in our philosophy we should strive to be consistent in our views. The teacher who professes to believe in the dignity of each individual but who engages in ridicule and derision of his students is guilty of building logic-tight compartments in his thinking which reflect an inconsistent philosophy.

These three criteria are difficult to separate from each other. No doubt their interrelation has already occurred to you. Indeed, it is most difficult to think about one without bringing the other two into consideration. We should not be concerned about this interrelation; the testing of our assumptions demands that all three be applied in the process.

Of additional interest in our study is the relationship of philosophy to other subjects. Disciplines other than philosophy have made contributions to the curriculum; they, too, have arrived at conclusions as to the nature, scope, and purpose of our educational efforts. It is important that we be acquainted with them and their relationship to philosophy. The disciplines of science, social science, and psychology have a particularly close relationship to the study of philosophy. All three have in common a faith in scientific thought as a means of achieving their desired ends. As opposed to philosophy their primary purpose is not the examination of assumptions but the establishment of factual knowledge.

There are many matters of common concern between the scientific and philosophic methods of inquiry. The scientist attempts to determine answers through research and experimentation; the philosopher depends on logic and reason. The assumptions of the philosopher often become the hypotheses to be tested by the scientist. The questions raised in epistemology and metaphysics in particular are common concerns of science and philosophy. The differences which exist are those of method rather than content.

Beyond this, however, philosophy and science have other relationships. The sciences rest on assumptions of a philosophic nature. The beginning of science is philosophy; indeed, we may speak of a *philosophy of science*. Such scientific ideals as skepticism and the search for proof are not themselves provable; they are philosophical ideals which the scientists accept in order to carry on their scientific explorations. In the study of chemistry, for example, one can prove a vast number of things about the nature and structure of matter; one thing that cannot be proved, however, is the value of such discoveries. This quest for value belongs to the philosopher. Science can create an atomic bomb—it cannot tell us how to use the bomb.

But as science makes new discoveries, it in turn affects philosophy. The creation of new scientific concepts of the nature of the universe causes the philosopher to reexamine his beliefs about metaphysics; the advancement of psychological information leads to reinvestigation in the field of epistemology. Thus science becomes not only the product of philosophic thought; philosophy also is modified by the product of scientific inquiry.

PHILOSOPHY AND THE CURRICULUM

Thus far in this discussion we have concentrated on the definition and description of general philosophy. We have not yet become involved in the philosophy of education or in the philosophic foundations of the curriculum. One may well ask how philosophy of education differs from philosophy as a whole. Is it a subdivision—as is logic or ethics—or is its relationship of a different sort?

The answer to this question put in its simplest terms is this: *Educational philosophy is not a separate area of philosophic thought; education is, rather, one area of life to which philosophic thought may be applied.* To attempt to separate educational philosophy from general philosophy is the same as to attempt to separate the automobile from the engineering which brought it into being.

No term in education is more misused today than the term *educational philosophy.* You may have seen credos hanging on the walls of principals' offices boldly titled, "Our Philosophy of Education." You may have also heard teachers' discussions of how many students will pass or fail labeled as educational philosophy. In both these cases, as well as in hundreds of others we could cite, such designation is erroneous. Actually, it is the assumptions that have been made, the guides to behavior that

17

have been developed, that should be called educational philosophy.

Let's look at it this way. Philosophy has provided us with significant insights into all areas of life. Some of these insights have particular importance to the way we teach our young; others are of minor or secondary importance; and still others have no relationship to education. In educational philosophy we are concerned with those concepts which have particular meaning and importance to the field of teaching and learning. In the strictest sense of the word, there is no such thing as educational philosophy. There is only philosophy which is applicable to education.

We should also be aware that the road between philosophy and education is a two-way street in the same way as that between philosophy and science. Not only does philosophic thought aid the educator as he makes the day-to-day decisions about the problems he faces, but philosophic thought may in turn draw heavily on the experiences and observations of the practitioner in acquiring the raw materials from which to build its systems. Philosophers seek to form their principles on the events of the real world, and the schools are an excellent source of such phenomena.

The term educational philosophy is a rather broad one. Our restriction of it to mean the application of philosophy to education still leaves us with an area of study which is vast and complex. We can apply philosophic thinking to school administration, to pupil transportation, hot lunch programs, or to the multitude of other aspects of education. Our efforts must be directed toward a more restricted area; we must narrow further the subject of our study.

It is wise to remind ourselves that the fundamental reason for the existence of schools is to forward the learning of individuals. The instructional role of the school—thus the curriculum—is at once the starting point and the end product of all we do in education. All the extra attachments and complexities of the educational system—administrative control, finances, transportation, etc. ad infinitum—exist only that the curriculum may exist. It therefore behooves us to focus our attention on the curriculum and instruction and to examine them in the light of philosophic thought.

Can such a study—the study of philosophic foundations of the curriculum—be of any real worth? We return to the question posed at the beginning of this chapter, "Is all this theory of any practical value?" Is there any value to the educator's or student's investigating the assumptions about the curriculum? Perhaps you are already convinced that such a study is of real worth, but there are specific practical considerations which are worthy of being cited.

The study of the philosophic foundations of the curriculum can help each of us achieve his own outlook—his own philosophy—which will establish guidelines for all of his practices. There can and should be a carry-over from his philosophic inquiry into all phases of the instructional program. Those who are concerned with education are continually plagued with questions and problems about what should be included in the curriculum. If such a person has not developed a sound philosophy —a philosophy which is at once reliable, valid, and consistent— he must make his decisions in terms of the expediencies of the situation. His decisions are, therefore, open to all the pitfalls that such practice permits. Conversely, with a set of consistent beliefs he is much more likely to arrive at sound answers to his problems.

Another service that the study of philosophic foundations of the curriculum can offer is to provide criteria for evaluating new methods and programs of education. At the present time the school is going through one of its most revolutionary periods. It is bombarded with new suggestions for school programs and new methods to improve the quality of education. Recent years have seen a deluge of reports from commissions and foundations advocating radical innovations for the schools. The teacher, as well as the layman, is confused by conflicting reports as to the worth of these various plans and suggestions. As an example, how about educational television? Is it the best means by which to educate the ever increasing school population? Or is it only "educational crop dusting?" Much is written and said about teaching machines or programmed learning. How effective is this technique? Is the learning so gained the kind we are seeking for our children? We could go on and on with such questions, but it is sufficient to say that most of our confusion is the result of our not having a consistent set of criteria to use in evaluating such innovations. If an individual does have such a philosophy, he can evaluate each new arrival to the educational scene with wisdom rather than with prejudices formed under the pressure of the moment.

The study of the philosophic foundations of the curriculum, then, can serve the very practical purpose of providing the means by which we can make the decisions required in the business of furthering progress in education.

Methods of Study

This book was written with the purpose of leading your thinking from one idea to the next in a logical sequence of steps so as to aid you in the development of your own philosophy of the curriculum. No attempt will be made to win you over to any particular point of view. The thinking and conclusions you reach as you read through this volume must be your own. No one can think for you; no one should tell you what conclusions you should reach. You will be shown some basic assumptions that may be made. You will be guided toward the critical examination of these so that you can eventually arrive at your own philosophy.

A common difficulty encountered by the student who first begins his study of philosophy is that he often gets bogged down in the terminology of the subject. Old words are used in new and different ways, and new words are introduced so rapidly that it is often staggering to the novice. However, this is an idea book rather than a word book. You will encounter new terms, but these will be brought to your attention only after the ideas they represent have been investigated. Keep the center of your interest focused on the development of your thinking and not on the words which stand for the ideas involved.

As a starting point for this approach, let us look at the curriculum itself. As we have noted, basic to all education is the curriculum; it is the core unit of the educational process. With the camouflage of extra school service that has grown in recent years, we are likely to lose sight of this central purpose of education. But it *is* the central purpose and as such is the best starting point for our considerations.

Let's begin by stripping the term "curriculum" of all superfluity and jargon. Let's ask ourselves what are the fundamental necessities for the existence of a curriculum?

First, there must be a *learner*—someone to build into his own being whatever is available to learn. Without the learner there would be no reason for the existence of education.

Next, there must be the *subject matter,* that is, the thing to be learned. In its broadcast definition it includes not only the knowledge of fact, but the skills, understandings, attitudes, and appreciations that the learner gains. Some teachers sneer at subject matter and make such meaningless statements as, "I don't teach subject matter, I teach children." But if there is nothing to learn, no learning can possibly take place.

Then there is the *learning process* itself, the way in which the subject matter is taken in by and becomes a part of the learner. This is a complicated process and, at best, is only partially understood by the psychologists and philosophers.

And, finally, there is the *teaching agency,* a subtle but necessary part of the whole learning procedure. Such an agency may fittingly be called the catalyst of the learning situation. The teacher is no more than a teaching agent, but even when there is no teacher present, there is an agency that guides, directs, and organizes the learning experience. The child who discovers a wild flower while alone in the woods and thereby learns does so because somewhere, someone, or something has directed and organized his thinking so that the learning could be achieved.

In its broadest aspects, the term teaching agency involves much more than schools and teachers. Included must be the society within which the child lives, with all its folkways, mores, and value systems. This society is a constant source of pressure on the individual to become a functioning member of the group. It is through the society, too, that the child becomes heir to the vast cultural heritage which has been accumulated through the centuries. In addition, every society perpetuates itself through its educational system and continually instructs the schools as to what it expects of them.

These four—these four and no more—ingredients make up the curriculum. And it is with these four factors that we work in our quest for a better understanding of our assumptions. Each of us has made assumptions about each of these elements whether he has done so consciously or unconsciously. The differences in our assumptions lead to differences in our beliefs and opinions, and these, in turn, lead to differences in curriculum practices. If a teacher believes his students to be mentally lazy and that he must continually apply pressure in order to get them to learn, he is making certain assumptions about the learner. If one decries the insufficient knowledge of geography possessed by today's young people, one is making assumptions about what subject matter should be learned. To state that the aim of education is to teach the child how to think reveals an assumption about the nature of the learning process. The critic who says today's teachers are overtrained in method at the expense of knowledge of subject matter is making an assumption as to the role of the teaching agency.

You have heard many such assertions as those in the preceding paragraph. However, those who make such statements are rarely aware of the assumptions that underlie them. In the chapters which follow, we will examine the four basic components of the curriculum in light of the different basic assumptions we can make about each. We will then see how the adoption of these different assumptions will lead to differences in educational practices.

As a nation we are now, and have been for the past ten years or more, engaged in what has been referred to as "the great debate about American education." Evidences of this debate are to be found all around us. Arguments rage as to what subjects should be included in the curriculum; people cry out that the schools are controlled by "eggheads," or by "educationists," or by "big business," or by "Reds." Charges and counter-charges are hurled by the educators, and the casual onlooker must be perplexed by the apparent sincerity and yet the vehemence of those engaged in the debate.

Few of us try to look beyond the dust of the battle, and thus more heat than light is produced by such debate. What is desperately needed is a deeper examination of the philosophies which are behind such arguments. Whether as a participant or as an onlooker, we should each be able to see beyond the immediate questions raised in this battle to the deeper underlying philosophic questions. It is true that at the philosophic level differences will be as great as they are at the surface level. Nevertheless, common areas of agreement can be found, and by dealing with issues at deeper levels we can come to tolerate differences in belief. If this book can do no more than stimulate philosophic thought about the great issues of the curriculum, it will be of value.

Thus we return to our original question as to the value of theory in its relationship to practice. If the study of philosophy can develop these insights of which we have spoken, we then will be able to say, "It is good theory *because* it works."

CHAPTER II

•

THE LEARNER

What better place is there to begin a study of the curriculum than with the learner? If the curriculum is the central concern of the school, then the learner is the central concern of the curriculum. For it is the student who is the raw material of the educative process, and it is also the student who is the finished product of the process. The child comes to school early in his life. The curriculum becomes a major factor in his growth and development; and it is by his knowledge, his abilities, his skills, and his attitudes that the curriculum of the school can and will be judged.

The assumptions we make about the learner will not only influence our behavior toward him; it will also determine the kind of curriculum we plan for him. Let us examine what this implies. Below are listed four statements about the curriculum; each is typical of a different viewpoint of the student as reflected in curriculum practices. As you read them, try to ascertain which comes closest to your own point of view and which you cannot accept.

1. It is best to set up standards of ahievement and require every child to attain them in order to pass the subject.
2. In teaching we should emphasize interest, creativity, and self-realization rather than mastery of content.
3. The ultimate outcome of all education should be to make the individual capable of adjusting to his physical and social environment.
4. The secret of successful teaching is to help the child study those things which his natural curiosity makes him want to explore and learn about.

The Learner

Each of these statements is typical of an attitude which reflects a certain philosophic assumption concerning the nature of the learner. As we study these theories you will come to realize that far more is implied by such statements than might at first seem evident. For all such statements we hear about teaching and the curriculum are reflections of different answers to a central question concerning the nature of man.

THE CENTRAL PROBLEM: WHAT IS THE BASIC NATURE OR PREDISPOSITION OF THE INDIVIDUAL?

Underlying all of the considerations as to the nature of the learner is the fundamental problem of his innate predisposition. This is to ask, "What is the nature of human nature?" Or to put it more simply, "What is the child like when he first arrives on this earth?" This is a critical question and the answer we give will determine not only our answers to questions such as those proposed at the first of this chapter but also the type of curriculum to be found in our schools.

Down through history philosophers have wrestled with the problem of the nature of man, and the answers they have found have proved to be of prime importance in determining the types of curricula which are to be found in our schools.

THE THEORY OF NATURAL EVIL

One of the earliest assumptions about the personality of the individual is that which can be titled *the theory of natural evil*. Like all such labeling, there is a danger that the nomenclature will carry with it connotations that are emotionally unacceptable. But when seen in its broadest context, the theory is one which has great appeal because of its emphasis on traditional values and outlooks.

In order to determine what is implied in this doctrine, it is necessary that we trace its historical development. The theory of natural evil is the oldest of the several doctrines which we will discuss in this chapter. Tracings of it are to be found in the philosophies of ancient Greece and Rome and in such medieval writers as Machiavelli (1469–1527). In its comprehensive form it emerged as a theological construct during the Middle Ages and the Reformation. This dogma held that man's need of salvation by God was the result of his (man's) own depravity. This state of man was the result of his fall from an idyllic state in Eden. Adam sinned and drove himself apart from God and thus became a creature of sin. Each of Adam's descendants became heir to his sin. In the New England Primer, *circa* 1785, this concept was expressed in this couplet:

> By Adam's fall
> We sinned all.

Thus all men are born into this world in a state of natural depravity or inborn evil. The individual's only hope is to surrender himself completely to God, to accept God's son Christ as an intermediary and thereby return to the state of Adam before his sinning.

With the emergence of the Age of Reason shortly before the French Revolution, men began to examine religion with the same searching scrutiny that they applied to all aspects of life. This examination led to the discarding of much of the mysticism that had been perpetuated by the church. The concept of natural evil was out of keeping with the newer view of man's relationship to God. Men struggled to find better answers to the question of man's basic nature. The results were often not an abandonment of earlier theories but a modification of them. One of the most common variations was that the child is a naive, stupid being whose selfish motives cause him to want to remain in his state of ignorance. But regardless of what adjectives were used to describe man, the same basic thesis appeared. This thesis was that the child is the least important part of the educative process; he is but the recipient; his wants, desires, and motives should be of little concern.

The basic construct of the theory of natural evil can be stated in these explicit terms: Each individual is born with a predisposition which is in exact opposition to all we attempt to do in education. It is the aim of education to make men good, knowledgeable, and wise. This aim is counter to the child's basic nature and motivation; for he seeks to avoid this knowledge and understanding. Education thus becomes a contest between the child, who is naive at best, evil at worst, and the teacher, who is attempting to force him to learn. Children by their nature are lazy, stupid, and undisciplined. Only by the application of strict discipline can the nature of the individual be changed so that he can develop those characteristics which are deemed admirable by the educator.

The acceptance of this theory is not at all difficult to find among educators. Evidence of this acceptance can be found in those teachers who subscribe to the idea that they must impose their authority on the children by making them learn what they (the teachers) deem to be of greatest value. The curriculum thus becomes entirely teacher-dominated and without consideration of the child's needs or interests.

The first of the four statements presented at the beginning of this chapter is a reflection of the theory of natural evil: "It is best to set up standards of achievement and require every child to attain them in order to pass the subject." For the belief that the individual must measure up to the expectation of some outside authority is the result of the assumption that the individual is incapable of setting his own levels of performance or evaluating his own efforts.

Such a conviction carries with it certain major inconsistencies or weaknesses. One of the most outstanding of these is that it relegates man to an inferior position. It assumes that the nature of human nature is such that men must learn to conform to some authority outside of their own ideas and feelings. Our democratic ideals are based on the direct opposite of this presupposition.

In its religious roots too, the theory of natural evil has one major inconsistency. Man's evil nature can only be regarded as part of his total being. If, then, man is the creation of God, we must accuse God of having created an evil thing. This logical inconsistency cannot be bypassed, and inasmuch as the religious dogma of natural evil was the forerunner of present day conviction, the whole structure of the persuasion seems to be on shaky grounds.

THE THEORY OF NATURAL GOOD

In the eighteenth century, a new creed rose to challenge the theory of natural evil. The gradual movement of men away from religion as the pivotal point of their existence caused them to seek other answers as to the basic nature of man. As we have seen, in some cases this resulted in a mere modification of the theory of natural evil; but in others men completely rejected the earlier concepts, and they began to seek a system of thought which would be more in keeping with the changing outlook of men toward their world and themselves.

The formulation of a comprehensive philosophy built around this new view of man was the product of a Frenchman, Jean Jacques Rousseau (1712–1778). As a forerunner of the French Revolution, Rousseau was one of the brilliant writers who gave to their period the name "Age of Reason." So revolutionary was his thinking that it attracted international attention in his own day and left a permanent mark on the history of philosophy.

Rousseau's first great point of departure from the theory of natural evil was in his proclamation that man's innate or basic nature is godlike. If children are the creation of a perfect divine being, he reasoned, then they could only be created as perfect as the creator himself. To view the newborn infant as anything other than perfect would be to ascribe this imperfection to the creator as well.

But it is obvious even to the most casual observer that if men are born good, they do not remain in this state of perfection. One need not view the derelict in the gutter or the murderer waiting in death row to be aware of this imperfection; each of us has enough self-knowledge to recognize his own foolishness, frailty, and weakness. If we were born good, what happened to us? What is the source of this evil, contaminating influence?

Rousseau found the answers to such questions in the influence of society on the life of the individual. He saw society as the perpetrator of all that is evil. Primitive man, he reasoned, was truly a noble creature, for he did not know this contaminating influence. But as man became more civilized, he had to learn to thwart his own good nature in order to survive in the society. He thus took on, perpetuated, and further developed the evils of the society.

To Rousseau, the hope of a good life lay in education, but this education must be of a particular sort. It must be planned to meet the wants and needs of the growing child; it must be free of the stifling influence of a predetermined curriculum; and it must have as its objective the free, simple life, uncluttered by the evil influences of social conformity.

The work of Rousseau, although highly influential in his own time and of great influence in the period immediately following, did not find continued popular acceptance. There are numbers of logical inconsistencies within it. (How can good men create an evil society?) In many cases it fails to be confirmed by reality. One has but to observe the behavior of very young children at play to see that they demonstrate but little evidence of unselfishness. They have little desire to share their toys or to consider the feelings of others.

But while the assumptions that Rousseau made tended to lose popularity, vestiges of this view began to find their way into the thinking and writing of later philosophers.

Today, there are many educators who feel that although Rousseau may have been overzealous in proclaiming the natural goodness of the individual, much of what was implied in his opinions was true and valuable. Anthropologists have emphasized the value of the simple, primitive society in providing the individual with a satisfying, socially rewarding existence. But of greater influence have been the psychologists who have promulgated the view of the child's stages of development as keys to understanding his needs. The concept that they have created is that each period of a child's life is marked by its own unique needs and developmental tasks. The key to successful curriculum planning, in their view, is in developing a curriculum centered around the real needs of children. Although this approach does not assume the child to be of godlike nature, it does leave the child in the position of being the ultimate criterion for the evaluation of all learning experiences.

Of still more recent development is the philosophy of Existentialism. Although this doctrine has been in the process of development for almost a century, it has been largely since World War II that its influences have been felt in education. Many Existentialists state that the philosophy is not a complete system but instead is a point of view. But regardless of differences in viewpoint among Existentialists and regardless of the complexities which Existentialism exhibits in its broader perspective, there are certain assumptions which underlie all Existential thought, and one of these is concerned with the nature of man.

Existentialism insists that each individual's chief duty is to himself—that the individual's greatest need is his own self-actualization. To use the words of Rollo May, "To the extent that we fulfill our potentialities as persons, we experience the profound joy to which the human is heir." Such a philosophy, even though it does not assume that the individual is innately good, is like earlier Rousseauism in that it places the individual at the apex of all philosophic considerations.

All of these beliefs agree on one central point, however. They see the human being as having an innate or natural predisposition toward those activities which are good for him and for the groups of which he is a part. The logical inference follows that the child knows best what is good for him, and that the idea source of curriculum materials and content is the child's own choice. The teacher who begins each day by saying, "Good morning, children! What would you like to do today?" is paying tribute to the belief in the natural goodness of the learner.

The key word in such a philosophy becomes "freedom." Freedom should be provided to the student to do whatever he desires, to say whatever he wishes, and to learn whatever he wants to learn. Conversely, the least desirable goal in education is conformity, for to direct the child or to force him to accept other people's values is to stifle his natural tendencies of creativity, his own natural interests, and his desire for the good life.

Should the teacher or curriculum worker find himself in support of the theory of natural good, what would be the resulting practices? What kind of relationships would he seek to build with his students? What kind of learning experiences would he provide for them? What type of curriculum would he advocate?

The obvious answers to these questions reside in the term *the child-centered school*. The term is more than one of convenience, for it implies a curriculum in which first considera-

The Learner

tion is given to the child's needs—*his* needs as *he* feels them. To refer again to the four statements which we listed at the beginning of this chapter, the second assertion that "in teaching we should emphasize interest, creativity, and self-realization rather than mastery of content" implies the natural goodness view of the nature of children. According to this view, only by removing the restrictions of a preset curriculum can the child enjoy the learning experiences which provide for his free, uninhibited growth. Forcing children to subscribe to a curriculum designed and built by adults can only bring about tensions, frustrations, and failures to achieve self-realization. The failure to provide an education which is based on the life needs of children is certain to result in unhappy, aggressive, emotionally disturbed individuals.

The following description (taken from *Newsweek* magazine) of a school where the philosophy of natural goodness is upheld will prove illuminating:

> If a youngster wants to swear in class (and some do), that is perfectly permissible. Little, in fact, is forbidden by the school code. . . . At one recent session, punctuated by laughs, burps, and shouts, a noisy debate developed over what to study: "I want geometry." "No, I hate math; let's have nouns and verbs." "I want to write a love story about goons."[1]

Such a school is a far cry from what most of us have experienced; but advocates of the child-centered curriculum maintain that we must look beyond the immediate situation to the ultimate values which will be inculcated by such a program of studies. Freed from the restrictions of adult imposed discipline, they say, the child will develop his own self-discipline; freed from the requirements for learning from a preset curriculum, the child will learn more because of his intrinsic motivation to learn; freed from the requirement to conform to his social role, the child will realize his full potential as a unique human being.

One weakness of the theory of natural good takes precedence over all others. This is its failure to take into considera-

---

[1]*Newsweek*, June 29, 1964, p. 83.

tion the social aspects of life and the cultural heritage. The curriculum of a school which is devoted to meeting the immediate felt needs of children can give no assurance of passing on the vast cultural background to which we are heirs or of helping the child to learn the give and take demanded by group living.

Indeed, it may be argued that man's most unique characteristic is his ability to profit from shared experience. Without this capacity to learn from past generations, human progress is impossible. To disregard this cultural heritage and to develop a curriculum which reflects the whim and caprice of the student would reduce man to the status of animalistic existence.

THE THEORY OF EVOLVING MAN

The theory of natural good which catapulted the individual into the central position in the universe did not long hold sway. For one thing, supporters of the theory found that the "brave new world" which they had envisioned did not come into being. This lack of reality of the theory was evidenced not only in the general social picture but also in the specifics of child-rearing practices and school programs. Practices growing out of these beliefs bordered on chaos. A new conception of the nature of man was demanded which would restore order out of the loose ends created by the theory of natural good.

Of more importance to the development of the new view of man was the advent of the Age of Science. This revolution in thinking brought with it the requirements that men be examined in the searching light of scientific inquiry; that we cast aside our metaphysical concepts and see men as atomistic beings in a vast and complicated universe; and that we study their behavior as being orderly and predictable.

The most radical departure from old ways of thought came with the publication of *The Origin of Species* by Charles Darwin (1809–1882). Published in 1859, this book, along with his *The Descent of Man,* proposed the thesis that man came into being out of eons of time and as a result of the process of survival of the fittest. Darwin viewed the individual not as a unique spiritual being but only as the product of a continual struggle for existence in which man had evolved characteristics which fitted him to survive in his present environment.

Darwin's theory of evolution did not remain the sole property of the biologists; others took the concepts and made them applicable to their areas of scholarship. Chief among those who adopted the theory was the English philosopher Herbert Spencer (1820–1903), who saw evolution as a social process in which cultures change in order to meet the demands of changing conditions. Society, reasoned Spencer, is like a biological species which struggles to maintain itself in a hostile environment. Those societies which are the fittest and best equipped to meet the challenge of these changing conditions will survive and perpetuate their folkways, mores, and laws. Those that cannot meet the challenge will decline and fall.

The Age of Science also brought with it the new science of psychology, which attempted to explain man's behavior in the same cold light in which his physical being had been examined by the biologists. Although different systems of psychology explained man's behavior in different ways, probably no single thinker's tenets received more widespread acceptance than those of Sigmund Freud (1856–1939). Freud presented a view of man as a complex being whose personality is ever evolving and changing. In this view our earliest childhood experiences set the patterns of our personality; we then spend all of our lives developing more complex behaviors which always relate to these earlier patterns. Freud's beliefs can thus be seen as reflecting an evolutionary view of the individual personality just as did Darwin's theory of the development of the biological species and Spencer's theories about the development of a society.

Each of these theories rests on a common assumption as to the basic nature of man, and it is from this assumption that we get the name for this view of the learner, *the theory of evolving man*. The fundamental construct is that the individual is no more than an adjusting, evolving piece of protoplasm. Man is neither good nor bad by nature, he simply exists. What the individual becomes is not the result of any innate predisposition but is the result of what he learns to become. The child evolves through experience; some of these experiences may be good in a social sense, others bad, but all produce learning, and through learning the individual develops the personality which is his at any given moment of his life. This theory puts learning in a truly exalted position. Learning becomes the way to achieve goodness——the avenue to desirable behavior. In a like manner, the self-centered man, the evildoer, the thief, and the murderer are also products of their learning experiences.

Curriculum practices can be inferred from the theory of evolving man just as in the previously discussed theories. Supporters of this theory would advocate a curriculum which would have as its main objective the development of those capacities which would make possible the student's adjustment to his ever changing environment. Curriculum content would neither be predetermined nor left to the whim of the student. Instead, the curriculum would have to be built around the real problems which people meet in day-to-day living.

If at the beginning of his chapter you selected the third statement, that "the ultimate outcome of all education should be to make the individual capable of adjusting to his physical and social environment," you place yourself among those who see the child as an evolving person who must continually adapt to an ever changing environment. You therefore perceive the ultimate objective of education to be that of bettering this adjustment.

Typical learning experiences in such a curriculum would be the study and discussion of contemporary social problems, laboratory experiences in which the individual becomes actively engaged in community affairs and in learning the intricacies of social adjustment within the peer group.

Another important implication of the theory of evolving man is that curriculum emphasis is on the method of problem solving rather than on the mastery of content. *What* the child learns is less important than *how* he learns; for ideally, the end product of education is the individual who has learned through his experience to solve his problems with maximum effectiveness. The child should learn how to recognize, define, and attack the problems of living.

The theory of evolving man has had its effects on education for only about fifty years. It has ever since been as violently attacked as any belief that has been promulgated. Perhaps the contentions strike too hard a blow at some of our religious values, or perhaps they are too coldly scientific. But there is a more basic inference which makes the theory unacceptable to many philosophers. This is the position that man is no more than a blade of grass that fights to retain its life in a crack in the sidewalk or a cockroach struggling to find food in a kitchen. Man is thus stripped of all dignity and purpose of living.

THE THEORY OF ASPIRING MAN

Our final view of man, that of man as an aspiring being is a product of the twentieth century. Two English philosophers, Alfred North Whitehead (1861–1947) and Bertrand Russell (1872–   ), were largely responsible for the formation of the theory which restores to the individual the dignity that science had tended to take from him. The position taken by these men gives to science as eminent a position as did the theory of evolving man but still ascribes to man characteristics which are regarded as laudable in a traditional system of values. In attempting a wedding of scientific thought and older concepts, such as "the dignity of man," this viewpoint becomes an eclectic one. But we should guard against concluding that this theory is but an attempt to pull together varying views; it is unique in its position, for it takes a completely new direction in its attempt to answer the riddle of human nature.

The basic concept of the theory of aspiring man can be stated in these terms: Each man is by nature neither good nor bad, but he is blessed with a desire or aspiration to seek growth and self-realization beyond his immediate needs. Each man has an inquiring mind—a desire to know. This appetite for learning is greater than the simple demands for adjustment. This is not to say that man is basically good—as is held by the theory of natural good. The theory of aspiring man says that there is an inborn force operating within each individual which causes him to rise above his own selfish and personal goals to broader horizons of intellectual insights and relevant judgments, as well as to the self-fulfillment that comes through service to others.

Evidences of man's being an aspiring creature are readily found. Two examples may prove helpful. Michelangelo, when asked to paint the ceiling of the Sistine Chapel, did not want the commission. Nevertheless, he was pressured to undertake the task and worked for four and one-half years to complete the ceiling alone. It was for him a long, difficult, and unpleasant task. It would have been easy for him to adopt an attitude of indifference and to have done a poor job of painting. But there was a force operating within him that would not let him do a poor job. He *had* to paint as well as he could. The result is one of the greatest works of art the world has ever known.

One need not confine oneself to the creative arts to find examples. A builder of a house may be tempted to use shoddy materials and poor workmanship; he may know that the owner will not discover the deficiencies for a long time to come. However, like Michelangelo, there is a force operating within him that causes him to want to do his best. The pressures of the immediate situation may cause him to take short cuts, but the fact that he possesses some desire to do his best is evidence of the aspiring nature of man.

The curriculum worker who supports such an assumption as to the basic nature of man will find himself advocating a curriculum which will give support to the view of the student as a seeker of truth. He would say that since children begin school with an insatiable appetite for learning, the curriculum should be viewed as a compilation of experiences which provide the child with an opportunity to feed this appetite and to sharpen it further so that he will continue in his quest for learning beyond the confines of the present situation.

For this reason the curriculum should be as broad as possible. The object of learning activities is learning for its own sake, and every effort should be made to make the curriculum as interesting and as meaningful as possible. Every learning experience should be open-ended, that is, it should lead to further and more challenging learnings rather than be regarded as a closed and terminated activity upon its completion.

The fourth statement presented at the beginning of this

chapter, "The secret of successful teaching is to help the child study those things which his natural curiosity makes him want to explore and learn about," is a reflection of the theory of aspiring man. The holder of such a belief sees the pupil as an aspirer for knowledge; the role of the teacher is deemed to be that of nurturing this magnificent characteristic.

The weaknesses of the theory of aspiring man are readily apparent. Like the theory of natural good, there is a certain lack of reality in the view of the individual as a noble creature striving to achieve unselfish goals for himself and his fellow man. Again, ordinary observation makes us aware that even if individuals are born with noble aspirations, something happens to most of them which destroys or inhibits the development of these admirable characteristics. Supporters of the theory state that the lack of observable high aspirations is the result of these aspirations being destroyed by environmental influences; but such an argument also implies that this appetite for learning is not an innate characteristic but is learned by living in an environment which is conducive to the development of the inquiring mind. The chief thesis of this theory is therefore open to charges of either lack of reliability or lack of internal consistency.

SUMMARY AND TERMINOLOGY

As you have read the discussions of these various views of man, you have undoubtedly found yourself arguing with some of the remarks, renouncing others, and embracing still others. This is as it should be, for the theories presented here are of broad scope and leave room for individual modifications and variations. We have attempted to include most, if not all, of the present day views of the learner. It is hoped that by spelling out these theories in detail you have been able to re-evaluate your own thinking about the nature of the learner as a key to curriculum construction.

In the first section of this chapter there were presented four statements about the curriculum from which you were asked to choose the one which was closest to your own feeling. As you read through the chapter you were undoubtedly aware of the restatement of these ideas within the greater context of the theory of man which was reflected in each. Perhaps the reading of this chapter has changed some of your ideas, perhaps fortified them. But—hopefully—you have reexamined them and now see them in a clearer light than you did previously.

However, to be completely accurate and honest, it is necessary for us to hedge at this point. We could easily infer that the relationship between philosophic belief as to the nature of the child and the resulting curriculum practices is a direct or one-to-one relationship (e.g., the concept that the child is by nature evil automatically leads to a curriculum of predetermined content and absolute standards of achievement.) Such is not the case, for there are other factors (to be discussed in later chapters) which also influence the type of curriculum which is evolved. In addition we would do well to remember that statements of philosophy are often not reflected in educational practice. Other factors such as emotional reactions, pressures of the society, and the learning gained through experience can modify a stated philosophy and the resulting educational practices.

As was indicated in the first chapter of this text, we have attempted to steer clear of the technical jargon of philosophy. Nevertheless, there are a number of terms which we should introduce now. Remember that names are matters of convenience, and that the ideas they represent are more important than the names with which we label them. Naming or labeling schools of thought is always dangerous. Not only do you force a huge range of differences into a single pigeonhole, but you also run the risk of using the names in ways which are offensive to those who support the views. In one sense, each philosopher creates his own system of labeling which he uses as descriptive of the concepts as he perceives them. The nomenclature presented here is (admittedly) the author's, and is therefore subject to criticism from anyone whose approach is different. Nevertheless, we should be familiar with the commonly accepted nomenclature of our field of study; so let us examine our theories from that viewpoint.

The theory of natural evil is a part of a greater and more comprehensive philosophy of the curriculum which carries the various titles of *Essentialism, Authoritarianism, Classicism,* or

Perennialism. The variety of names indicated here stems from aspects of the philosophy other than that of its view of the learner, however, for all of these have the common belief that by nature the student is a fugitive from learning.

The theory of natural good belongs with a philosophy of the curriculum known as *Idealism* or *Romanticism.* Although the term "Romanticism" has a shortcoming in that it has too many different meanings and connotations, it is still usable for our purposes here. The term "Idealism" is more widely used to express the postulate that the individual is by nature predisposed toward goodness and truth.

The theory of evolving man belongs to a philosophic school which is known variously as *Pragmatism, Instrumentalism,* and *Experimentalism.* The terms are interchangeable when used to describe the nature of the learner, for all of these carry the concept of the child as a growing, developing organism in a state of continual struggle in an environment which demands his constant adjustment to it.

The theory of aspiring man belongs with the philosophy called *Realism* or *Neo-Realism.* In its entirety the philosophy is a comprehensive, complex set of assumptions, but our concern here is only for its concept as to the nature of the child. And that is the belief that the individual is born with the desire to seek out that which is true and good.

In later chapters we will investigate the other components of the curriculum and will relate these to the theories we have described here. For the existence of the curriculum depends on the presence of all of these ingredients—learner, subject matter, learning process, and teaching agency.

CHAPTER III

•

THE SUBJECT MATTER

In 1592, Francis Bacon wrote a letter in which he made his often-quoted statement, "I have taken all knowledge to be my province." In the sixteenth and seventeenth centuries the "all knowledge" of which Bacon wrote was not nearly so vast an area of possible investigation as it is today. Even so, such an assertion was boastful even in Bacon's day, and he was of course never successful in achieving his ideal. Indeed, he remained woefully ignorant of some of the more important scientific thinking of his own time. Today, the totality of human knowledge—of what men know—has become so vast that any single individual can do little more than scratch the surface. In the last quarter of a century there has been an explosion of knowledge unequaled by the much discussed population explosion or any other growth phenomenon of our time. And it is safe to assume that the next quarter century will present an even greater growth of knowledge.

The learnings of any individual may be referred to as the subject matter of a learning experience. The questions to be answered are, "What shall we teach?" or "By what criteria shall we select the learnings to which we introduce the student?" With all the alternatives made possible by the increase in knowledge we must somehow decide what shall be learned—what things are most important to teach. Is it more important to teach the child to read or to get along with other children? Is it more useful to teach a high school student to scan a sonnet or to drive a car? What languages should a person be able to use, what scientific concepts should he understand, what history should he know, what vocational skills should he possess?

Obviously, we cannot teach every child everything; we must somehow find some way to select those things which are the most important, the most vital in the life of the child.

The situation is further complicated by the fact that there is not agreement within the fields of knowledge. Conflicts often appear between the various schools of thought within the same field. As an instance, much has been written and said lately about the teaching of communism in our schools. Should the social studies instructor teach about this enemy of our way of life, or should this be omitted for fear that we may poison the minds of our youth? And in teaching about our own way of life, should we make students aware of its weaknesses as well as its strengths? Should we make students aware of the vast complexities and often divergent views present within our own social order? Shall we teach them that socialism is an economic evil? If so, how shall we explain such socialistic American institutions as the post office and our highway system? Should the history teacher approach the study of the Mexican War as a heroic mission to save the people of Texas from the oppression of Mexico? As an imperialistic adventure of the United States? As an attempt by the South to strengthen its legislative position by securing more slave states?

How difficult our task is! We must somehow determine what should be learned from the vast quantity of material from which we can select. And we must do so in the clear recognition of the conflicts which exist between the disciplines and within the disciplines.

If a teacher is asked what he has taught during the past week, he will probably be able to give a fairly accurate listing of the subject matter he has presented to his students. If, however, he is asked *why* he presented this subject matter rather than some other, he will probably be unable to give answers without considerable thought.

What are some of the answers we might get to our question? They would probably be highly variable but would fall under four main headings.

Some teachers would reply that they teach certain things because they are in the textbook or in the state course of study. If we pursued the answer further, we would probably get a statement something like this: "The men who write textbooks and courses of study are experts in their fields. They know of the developments within their fields and are aware of the present trends and research. In following their plans we have the advantage of expert opinion. They are better equipped than is the classroom teacher to determine what subject matter should be included." Thus we arrive at one of the most frequently used criteria in the selection of content, that of *authoritative opinion*.

Curriculum content may be selected for other reasons. Frequently the teacher may include certain learning experiences simply because the students enjoy the work. Most teachers like to teach things which the students like to study; few will teach those things that the pupils find uninteresting or boring. Many teachers believe that the entire curriculum can be built on the interests and desires of the children, but even the teacher who does not go to such extremes includes some subject matter simply because his students react to it with enthusiasm. This criterion for the selection of subject matter may be referred to as the *felt needs* criterion.

A teacher might also include certain content because of a recognition of the *adult needs* of the learner. Spelling skills may be taught because of the recognition that the adult in today's world is much better off if he possesses such skills. In vocational education the primary determiner of the curriculum content is the requirements of the world of work. Other examples could be cited, but these are sufficient to describe what is meant by the criterion of adult needs.

Finally, some subject matter is selected because of its value as a tool for *future learnings*. The elementary teacher who teaches reading skills to his pupils does so, not so much because the ability to read is of great importance in itself, but because of the recognition that future school success depends on the child's reading skill. In like manner all advanced learning depends on the mastery of content of a more fundamental nature. All teachers are deeply aware of this criterion for the selection of subject matter content; one of their most fundamental concerns is that they send their students to the next level of learning adequately prepared.

These four criteria are probably used by all teachers to some degree. In a practical sense such criteria are not only useful but are philosophically sound. Each rests on a set of assumptions related to the nature of the curriculum.

Although we may use any or all of these criteria in selecting subject matter, we do not really get to the heart of the question of why we should or why we do select certain subject matter from the vast quantities which are available. We still must face our basic question, "What determines what we should teach?"

Let's try to get the problem into a more manageable form. If we can, let's try to establish some general assumptions which we can all accept and then develop our varying views in terms of these generalities.

A good starting place is the fact that we can all accept the idea that we should teach the child those things which are true, good, and of greatest value. Certainly we do not want to teach facts or doctrines which we know to be false. Our job of selection now becomes one in which we attempt to identify those parts of the subject matter which are true and of greatest value.

Accepting this reinterpretation of our problem, however, brings us to a new one—now we must judge what is true and of greatest value. In their attempts to find solutions to this problem, philosophers are in disagreement, and these disagreements produce differences in curriculums. The assumptions which the philosophers make as to the nature of truth serve as keystones to the structure on which answers to our other questions can be built. So let us look at the more prominent theories —theories of truth and value—and see their implications for educational practice.

THE CORRESPONDENCE THEORY OF TRUTH

The correspondence theory of truth refers to agreement or likeness. If your opinion and mine are the same—that is, if they agree—they may be said to correspond.

Now, to advocate the correspondence theory is to hold that the knowledge we have of a thing (i.e., a fact, an event, a concept, etc.) is like the thing as it really is. Men once thought that the earth was flat. This knowledge, however, did not correspond with the real or true shape of the earth; it was, therefore, according to this theory, a false belief or learning.

In applying this theory we must ask ourselves, "Does the thing we are teaching correspond or agree with reality?" Choices of subject matter can then be made on the basis of their conformity to the realities of the world around us.

Let's see how this works. Take as an instance Newton's law of universal gravitation. Is it true or not? Since it conforms or agrees with the universe as it actually is, it may be said to be true and is, therefore, worthy of being handed down from generation to generation by way of the teaching-learning situation. Applying the same reasoning to the old idea of the flatness of the earth would lead us to discard that idea.

Put in other terms, the assumption made by this theory is that the *truth* exists outside of and independent of the knowledge of it. The extent of agreement of our knowledge with the actual thing as it exists in the real world is the extent of the truthfulness of our knowledge.

In dealing with scientific fact we can see the application of the correspondence theory of truth in its purest form. In other fields we run into more involved applications, however. An English teacher might be concerned with whether Longfellow or Whitman is more deserving of study by the pupils. Is the poetry of Longfellow *truer* than the poetry of Whitman? Can we say with certainty that either is the better poet? Fifty years ago Longfellow was considered by the critics to be our greatest American poet, while Whitman was hardly noticed; twenty years ago the positions were reversed, Whitman was praised, Longfellow was considered second-rate; recent years have once more seen a resurgence of Longfellow's popularity. Which author is truly the greatest and worthy of the most study? Here our correspondence theory of truth does not give us adequate guidance. Actually, much of what the poet writes can make no claim to being either true or false. The poet is dealing with communication; his task is to relate his own emotional reactions to the reader in such a way that he (the reader) will share the poet's emotional experiences. If he succeeds in this effort, he will be a good (true?) poet.

Or let us take a statement such as, "Honesty is the best

policy." Is this a *true* statement? Does it correspond or agree with reality? Maybe so, maybe not. Is the honest man more likely to get material rewards for his honesty? A look around your own community will cast grave doubts. Are there other rewards—happiness or a sense of well-being—which come to the honest man? Maybe so, maybe not. Again our correspondence theory of truth needs further clarification. Perhaps such statements as, "Honesty is the best policy," are actually not to be regarded as either true or false. Some are expressions of opinions or assumptions, others are descriptions of situations, and still others are assertions which the perceptive observer has found to be accurate for him in that they have been verified by his own experiences.

All realities or truths are not of the same order. There is a difference between such statements as, "Eggs cost sixty-nine cents a dozen," and, "In a right triangle the square of the hypotenuse is equal to the sum of the squares of the other two sides." Statements that are descriptive of situations which may vary from time to time and place to place—such as the price of eggs or opinions of literary worth—are properly called *facts* rather than *truths*. Truths have the characteristic of being *absolute*—that is, they are true regardless of time, place, or circumstances. The Pythagorean Theorem and Newton's law of universal gravitation fit this characteristic and are therefore truths. To the believer in the correspondence theory it is these absolutes that are of major importance in philosophic considerations. And to the educators who support the theory, the content of the curriculum is easily defined by teaching the students these truths.

Here, however, we strike another snag, for we must know how to separate the absolute truths from fact and opinion. Regardless of the soundness of our logic up to this point, all of our efforts are useless unless we can separate the wheat from the chaff.

Unfortunately, there is no pat answer to this problem. It is at this point that, even among themselves, supporters of the correspondence theory come to a parting of the ways, for while they all support the importance of finding and governing one's life by the absolutes, they are in disagreement as to the source of these truths. The sources that are given are many, but for our purposes we should investigate several of the more significant ones.

The divine revelation theory is a religious concept that holds that God periodically reveals Himself to man. The manner and content of such revelation may be highly variable; it may be in the form of the writing of laws on tablets of stone or of the visitation by some angelic messenger or voice in the night. Such revelations are the source of truths on which principles of living should be based. They should be passed on from generation to generation with the young being thoroughly indoctrinated into their content and application. Unfortunately, the supporters of this view have never arrived at a criterion for separating the divine revelations from the hallucinations of madmen.

Essentialism strives for a more practical view. To the essentialist the truth is an evolved thing which man has discovered and is continuing to modify through his own intelligence and effort. The great truths of the universe are found by man's own intelligent quest for them. Each generation, building on the discoveries of the past generations, goes on to discover more and more about the world in which we live. The term essentialism is applied to this school of thought because as an educational view it emphasizes the essentials or fundamentals. This emphasis is the outgrowth of the idea that progress comes through individuals' being thoroughly grounded in the knowledge of the past so that they may make their contribution to the expansion of man's knowledge of the great, lasting, absolute truths.

I am certain that some informed readers will be somewhat chagrined at this description of the essentialist point of view. They will insist that rather than defining essentials in terms of absolute truths, the essentialist is as likely to define essentials as tested but still tentative truths. Although such a viewpoint is possible, the adoption of it comes dangerously close to removing the holder of it from the essentialist's camp and placing him in that of the pragmatist. (See below, p. 53).

Classicism, sometimes referred to as Perennialism, looks to the learnings that have stood the test of time as the source of knowledge of truths. In any period of man's history a multitude of ideas and concepts are expressed by tongue and pen. Of these very few live beyond their own time. Why? The classicist claims that few of man's expressions contain insights into the significant aspects of reality. Those ideas which do not have some quality of truth about them fail to live while those few ideas that possess this insight into ultimate and absolute truth live on from generation to generation. The classicist is unconcerned with how some men gain this insight and others do not; the vitality of any writing or thinking beyond its time of origin is proof enough of its worth. How can one explain the current vitality of the works of Plato, or Cicero, or Milton unless they contain something which met man's quest for certainty down through the ages? These works *must* hold some gems of truth that are absolute and lasting.

The truths which the classicist finds may be beyond his own power to verbalize; indeed, it is often impossible to construct exact statements of them. Such proverbs as, "Honesty is the best policy," are inadequate attempts to express the meaning and significance of honesty, but those thoughts of man that have stood the test of time contain the true ideas of honesty that are of lasting value.

As could be expected, educators who support this classical view would stress curriculum content of a traditional nature. The works of authors of bygone days, historical materials, and traditional values would be given prominence, for such subject matter has the advantage of having proved itself in the passage of time.

Closely allied with the classical view—though somewhat more restricted—is the view referred to as *humanism*. Humanists look to the works of man as containing or as being representative of the good, the true, and the beautiful. Down through the centuries, they say, the mind and the spirit of man have been able to develop their own insights into the eternal values and truths. The proof of these values is to be found in the fact that the great ideas and precepts are continually recurring in the great works of man. The discovery and rediscovery of these truths are not the province of the ordinary individual, however. They are the products of certain great men who had greater intelligence, more perceptive powers, and greater insights. As a result, these men could come to grips with these truths, examine them, and record them for posterity. Following this reasoning, the humanistic scholar values the best thinking of the best minds of history. The humanist supports the selection of "the one hundred great books" or "the great ideas of the Western world" as the proper avenue through which the individual may search for truth and thereby become an educated man.

Each of the schools of thought discussed in the preceding paragraphs looks to a different source to find the ultimate authority for truth. Yet they all have a common element within them; they all hold to the idea of absolute and ultimate truth, truth which exists outside of and independent of the individual. The difference in the view of a Communist and of a Roman Catholic is solely in their belief as to where the ultimate authority is to be found. The Communist looks to the Marxist dialectical theory as the source of truth; the Roman Catholic to the word of God as expressed through the teachings of the Catholic church. Both see the individual as finding his proper place by subservience to the proper authority.

When we attempt to discover the educational implications of this theory, the particular subject matter believed to be most important by its adherents may differ, but their general attitude toward the subject matter will always be the same. Believers in divine revelation will support religious instruction; essentialists, the development of fundamental skills and knowledge; classicists and humanists, the historical study of the classics in literature, art, and music. But regardless of what is given major consideration, the principal concept held by all is that there are certain things in the subject matter that the individual *must* learn. Their assumption is that there must be something inherently good in the subject matter that is studied; the individual wants, needs, and desires of the student are of secondary importance. They would all hold that the true values are in the things learned, for through them comes the knowledge of the absolute, ultimate values and truths.

Thus far we have seen this correspondence theory of truth only in terms of its meanings and applications to education.

But in a larger context there is much to recommend the theory when one considers its apparent logic and certainty. It makes for a simple, easy to follow way of life; one has but to find the absolute, ultimate truth and conform to its authority.

There are, however, major weaknesses or limitations to such a theory. The chief weakness is a logical one. How can we know if what we believe and what we teach correspond with reality? We cannot unless we can know reality or truth *directly*. And if we know reality or truth directly, then why do we need to be concerned with *belief*?

An example might be helpful here. If a stranger shows you a picture of a woman and asks you if you think it a good likeness of his wife, you could only answer that you do not know since you do not know his wife personally. The same reasoning applies in the correspondence theory of truth. If we cannot know the truth directly, how can we ever know the accuracy of our belief about the truth?

There is another weakness of the correspondence theory that is related to the first but is different in its application. Put in its simplest terms, it may be stated in the form of a question: "If there is no agreement as to the source of truth, how can we be sure that one authority is any truer than another?" We are so accustomed to taking certain authorities for granted that we seldom question assumptions back of our beliefs. Let us suppose a visitor from another planet who is totally unaware of our society and its value system was suddenly introduced to our culture. Suppose that he has had no early training to prejudice him toward believing in any earthly authority or source of truth. How confused he would be by the conflicts he would encounter! So many different "absolutes"—each claiming to be the ultimate authority of truth in the universe! Our visitor would probably resign himself to never being able to know which authority to accept. Any person who has thought deeply about the various assumptions of his own life is in much the same predicament; the debate among the supporters of the correspondence theory causes us to be skeptical of the theory itself.

Nevertheless, the correspondence theory of truth is probably the most widely accepted concept of those which we will study. You may find it an adequate explanation of the nature of truth.

If you do, you are with the majority. Many outstanding educators adopt such a view. But if the correspondence theory seems
inadequate to you, then you must search for other assumptions.

THE INTUITIVE THEORY OF TRUTH

If you were asked whether democracy is a better way of life than
communism, you would be likely to reply, "Undoubtedly!" If
asked why, you would answer in terms such as "the dignity of
man," or "the belief in freedom." If pursued further and asked
why these things are good, you would probably eventually say
something like, "Well, I don't know why democracy is better—I
just *know* it is, that's all!" Such a statement indicates a belief in
intuitive theory of truth, for the intuitive theory holds that
truth is not a thing to be arrived at logically but by an internal
awareness of the rightness or truthfulness of the belief under
consideration.

The intuitive theory holds that the truth or value of a
belief can only be tested in terms of our internal awareness of
it. Each person, it is believed, has an inborn capacity to dis-
tinguish the true from the false, the beautiful from the ugly,
and the significant from the trite. This God-given gift can be
applied to any situation at any time with a clear awareness
within the individual as to the rightness or wrongness of any
belief or anticipated action. This ability is referred to as *intuitive* in order to separate it from *logical* inasmuch as the ability
is the result of introspection of internal feelings rather than of
thought processes and reasoning.

There are many examples we could give of the application
of this intuitive theory, but the simpler ones are the best. Let
us suppose someone asks you a riddle or a thought-twister. If
you are able to figure out the solution, you do not have to be
told that your answer is the right one; you *know* it as soon as
you figure it out. How can this be accounted for? According to
this theory, only by your having an intuitive awareness of the
rightness of your answer.

Another example is that we may hold a concept of perfection which we have never experienced. For instance, all of us
know what a perfectly constructed circle would be like; we can
carry a mental concept of the figure. But such a thing has never

and will never exist. No matter how carefully we draw a circle, it will be imperfect in some detail. Thus we are aware "in our minds" of something that does not exist in the real world. We can intuitively know things which we can never experience directly. Truth can be arrived at, then, without reference to any exterior existence.

How, then, can we judge the truth of a belief or a teaching? According to the intuitive theory the truth can only be known if we *feel* that it is true. Man himself is held to be, in a sense, the source of truth. A thing may be judged as true when it conforms to our internal awareness of what is true. An act is right when it feels right; a belief is true when we inwardly know it to be true; an emotion is trustworthy when it carries with it a sense of well-being. There is in every man this awareness, and it alone is criterion enough to test any truth.

The curriculum practices growing out of the intuitive theory of truth are more difficult to trace than those which are derived from the correspondence theory. Indeed, even though we might accept the basic principles of the theory, we are likely to be left "up in the air" when attempting to put theory into practice in a classroom situation.

Primarily, the educational practices that grow out of the theory are tied to one basic premise, the need to encourage the further development of the student's intuitive powers. How can this be done? Educators who support this view put emphasis on the more aesthetic aspects of the curriculum. Subject matter areas such as art, music, and literature are given a primary role in the child's school life, but these are not taught by the traditional, historical approach nor by confining the child with rules and standards. The child must be freed from these restrictions so that his intuitive sense may develop as it can and should. Those who advocate the intuitive theory of truth object to the present day curriculum because it gives importance to the historical and classical aspects of the subject matter, thus stifling the child's creative potential by the pressures of conformity. They believe that the best subject matter is that which is selected out of the spontaneous interests and felt needs of the child.

But like the correspondence theory, the intuitive theory is

not without its limitations. Difficult—indeed, unanswerable—questions are certain to arise with the acceptance of the theory. First, there is the question of *differences*. How can we explain the fact that two diametrically opposed views may be held by two individuals and each of these individuals has intuitive feelings which convince him of the rightness of his belief? Moslems are as certain that their religion is right and true as are Christians. Communists are as certain of the rightness of their political and economic theory as are the supporters of our own way of life. These differences cannot be explained away by the supporters of the intuitive theory. That these differences exist is certain, and if the intuitive of the individual is infallible, we end with as many ideas of truth as there are individuals.

A second major weakness is that of *error*. Many times we feel intuitively that a thing is true which is later proved to be false. Probably every individual has at one time believed something to be true with a certainty he would be willing to stake his life on and then found he was wrong in what he believed. How can we explain this if the intuitive knowledge of truth is infallible?

Look at these two drawings:

Intuitively, you would accept that one line is longer than the other. But it can be easily proved that this is an optical illusion and that the lines are of equal length. The intuitive feeling is therefore not to be trusted.

In spite of its weaknesses, the intuitive theory of truth has many followers, particularly in the field of the fine arts, and it is there that it has made its major contribution.

There is another manner in which the intuitive theory has left its imprint. It has caused virtually all of the other philosophies to examine the intuitive bases of their own views. Most philosophers who would not classify themselves as supporters of the intuitive theory of truth admit that they must accept intuitive thought as being present—at least to some extent—in their own viewpoints. Supporters of the correspondence theory must admit that the individual must somehow be aware that he has found the source of absolute truth; and for this awareness he must depend on his internal sense of "rightness." The supporters of the pragmatic theory (see below) must admit to an intuitive awareness of the existence of problems and their resolution.

THE PRAGMATIC THEORY OF TRUTH

The present Age of Science has brought forth still another theory of truth. This theory, called the pragmatic theory, puts stress not on the *source* but on the *results* of truth. This set of assumptions begins by discarding all concepts of ultimate or absolute truth. To the pragmatist such ideas are only meaningless words assigned to concepts that no one understands. For him, to try to find the source of truth is a useless search. Truth can be found only in terms of whether a belief works or not. To the scientist in the laboratory this idea is his stock in trade. He cares little about absolutes; he sets up his hypothesis and then attempts to prove it. If it can be proved—if it works—he has established a scientific fact or principle. If it proves false—if it doesn't work—then he discards it.

The pragmatic theory of truth holds that the test of truth is to be found in the here and now of human experience. If a thing aids human experience, it is true; if it thwarts and stifles experience, it is false.

Some examples might prove helpful. Let us look at the way a pragmatist would approach some questions of truth and value. Is Hinduism a *true* set of religious beliefs? Certainly, he would say, it is based on the idea of absolute truth; and the emerging ideas are logically sound. But the Hindu religion is also responsible for the caste system of India; so regardless of any other criteria, the pragmatist would reject Hinduism because it results in a stifling of individual opportunity for growth.

Is honesty a desirable characteristic? The pragmatist would say that it may be established that only by being honest with each other can men hope to live together in peace and happiness. Therefore, he would accept honesty as a desirable characteristic regardless of any predetermined ideas about honesty as an absolute virtue.

It will be noted that when a pragmatist thinks of truth he does not think of it as being ultimate. To him an idea or belief may be perfectly true under one set of circumstances and not true under another set of circumstances. For instance, monogamy is regarded as the best system of marriage in European countries; but in the Arab world, polygamy is thought to be the best. In most circumstances killing another human being is regarded as wrong, but in the event of war it is encouraged. If we attempt to set up universal truths, say the pragmatists, we have to make exceptions so that in reality we do not have universal truths at all. Is it not sounder, they ask, to guide one's life by relative values rather than by absolute values that do not really exist?

Relative values are to be defined in terms of what they are relative to. In the pragmatic theory of truth all values are relative to human experience. The individual's ability to control and govern his own experiences is the criterion by which all truth is to be measured.

There are various ways in which this criterion may be applied. Some pragmatists put emphasis on a *personal* basis. In evaluating any belief or anticipated action they ask, "What will it do for me?" If the belief will aid the individual in understanding and controlling his own future experiences, it must be considered true and good; if it will inhibit this understanding, it should be discarded.

Other pragmatists assign importance to a *scientific* outlook. They believe that the key question that must be answered by any belief is, "Is it a usable hypothesis?" Adopting the attitude of the scientist, they use this criterion in facing all of life's problems. They believe that when seeking to find solutions to the problems which we face, we must create hypotheses, test them, and only if they prove usable, make them guides to action.

The pragmatic theory of truth has had great impact on our American school systems. The educational practices growing out of the theory have been particularly noteworthy because they are in such contrast to those of the correspondence theory. Whereas the correspondence theory would emphasize a curriculum based on the great, time-proven aspects of man's cultural heritage, the pragmatic view places little or no value on these things as such. Instead of the cultural heritage, the pragmatist puts his stress on the here and now of living. Courses which center in problem solving are regarded by them as being of greatest value. Study of the cultural heritage would be encouraged only when it would be useful in helping the student solve problems which are real and meaningful to him. Pragmatists advocate the abolition of traditional subjects of the curriculum. They see the ideal school as being a place where students are guided through problem solving experiences. As subject matter is needed to solve these problems, it is brought in to the learning situation to help with the solution. Through this procedure the student will learn more subject matter because he has tested the truth of the subject matter through his own experience.

Critics of the pragmatic theory are not without argument. There are weaknesses and limitations to the theory. The chief criticism that can be leveled at the theory is its lack of ultimate goals. As has been pointed out, the pragmatic theory sees the individual's experience as being the measure of all things. One may well ask whether human experience is end enough in itself to justify educational effort. If we say that growth is an end in itself, we must ask, "Growth toward what?" Surely growth implies direction—human experience must be measured in terms of some goal. This lack of direction—this lack of goals beyond the problems of here and now—tends to rob man of his dignity.

Another criticism that may be leveled against the pragmatic theory of truth is that it tends to produce people who are entirely self-centered in their outlook. Inasmuch as the individual's experience is raised to such a prominent position, we are likely to overlook the experiences of other people or of the group as a whole. An experience might be quite profitable to one individual but might prove harmful to those around him. It would not be difficult to imagine a situation in which the enrichment of one's own experience would in turn frustrate the personal growth of those around him. For example, a student could cheat on a test and thereby assure his success in that experience, but the other students, who play fairly, may suffer when they are compared to him; and society may suffer by giving him a position of responsibility for which he is not prepared. In putting all emphasis on the value of individual experience, it is argued by critics, you will create adults whose only standard of value is their own self-gratification.

THE COHERENCE THEORY OF TRUTH

In their quest to find a theory of truth that is at once broad enough to encompass all areas of human experience and still practical enough for individual application, some philosophers have turned to the coherence theory of truth. As a starting point, advocates of this theory make several new assumptions. Truth is viewed as not being confined either to certain forces outside of man or to within man himself. Instead, truth is viewed as existing everywhere in the universe. Truth exists within man and everywhere outside of man; truth is universal. Indeed, truth can be regarded as synonymous with reality; truth is nothing less than the totality of the universe. And since the universe is infinite in its proportions, they say, the truth is infinite.

According to this theory, inasmuch as the mind of the individual has finite dimensions, it follows that this infinite truth is out of reach of the individual. But although man's mind is finite, it does have the potential of growing in its knowledge of truth. The mind is viewed as continually extending itself—forever pushing back the horizons of its own knowledge.

An illustration of this point of view can be made here. Let us imagine a point of light on a plane of darkness that stretches on to infinity in every direction. The point of light represents man's knowledge; the plane of darkness, reality or truth of which he is ignorant. As man learns, the point of light becomes a larger and larger circle. As the diameter of the circle of light increases, however, the circumference of darkness also increases. Thus the learning individual becomes increasingly aware of the vastness of the darkness—of what he does not know. Further, since the darkness is infinite, regardless of the extension of the circle of light, there can be no hope of achieving total light.

To equate truth with reality would cause us to see truth in a much broader view than in any of the other theories we have thus far discussed. Truth would be found in the journey work of stars or in a single leaf of grass.

How, then, can the advocates of the coherence theory explain errors? If truth is to be found in all things, it would appear that there can be no such thing as a false belief; there is, however, belief which is incomplete and therefore subject to error. They look at it this way. If our knowledge of any subject is limited, we are much more likely to misunderstand what we encounter in dealing with that subject. The existence of our error is explainable not by something within the subject matter but in our own inadequacy of perception.

Therefore, they would say that our task is that of determining the adequacy of our belief—that is, whether our beliefs and teachings are complete enough to warrant our continuing to hold to them. The test to which we may put these beliefs is whether they are consistent with other beliefs accepted as true. We may accept a statement as being true if it "coheres" with other truths of which we are aware—thus the name, the coherence theory of truth. If we accept the assumption that the universe is in its entirety the totality of truth—and hence is an orderly, consistent creation—then each belief is true to the extent that it coheres or fits in with all other statements accepted as true.

An example may be helpful. Let us suppose a person stoutly maintains that the earth is flat. To support his view he quotes a scriptural passage describing the "four corners of the earth" and similar illustrations. Regardless of how much evidence he may summon to support his contention, we would reject it because it does not cohere with all the other truths we know about the shape of the earth.

In the early part of this chapter mention was made of the expanding sum of human knowledge—the "explosion of knowledge." To the supporters of the coherence theory of truth this explosion of knowledge presents no problem. It is, instead, a desirable thing, for it presents man with a greater opportunity in his quest for greater knowledge of the truth.

There is no greater good to the advocates of the coherence theory than the continual search for knowledge. The unfortunate characteristic of modern life and education is that they tend to dull rather than to sharpen man's appetite for learning. This is particularly true when the curriculum is based on one of the other theories discussed, for all of them are based on the selection of certain subject matter to the exclusion of other subject matter. The coherence theory of truth opens the door to *all* subject matter since all may lead to a growth of knowledge.

One qualification is needed here, however. To say of this theory that it states that all knowledge is of equal value is not precise. While there is value in all knowledge, some has a greater potential to lead to further knowledge. As an example, skill in reading will contribute more to one's future learning than will skill in building sand castles. Believers in the coherence theory of truth assign first importance to those learnings that increase the individual's potential for further and greater learning. The ideal of continued learning is thus upheld.

The curriculum implications of the theory are easily determined. Indeed, any learning would be regarded by it as good inasmuch as it would play its part in the individual's expanding horizons of knowledge. The curriculum would have no boundaries. All learning would be of value because all learning aids the individual's growth of knowledge and understanding. Ideally, the curriculum of the school would be characterized by unlimited breadth of subject matter. No attempt would be made to create a hierarchy of subjects in the school. Rather, all subjects would be accepted as being of value in the education of the individual. The only exception to this statement was noted previously; that is, some learnings tend to be more productive in that they lead to other learnings. Therefore these learnings would be given greater prominence in the curriculum.

As you might expect, the coherence theory of truth has its limitations. Chief among these is its lack of discrimination in what is to be learned. One could argue that it is just as valuable to learn the batting averages of baseball players as to learn the multiplication tables. Inasmuch as *all* learning is glorified, there is no criterion by which one learning can be judged against another. Using the coherence theory could lead to a curriculum that is a hopeless hodgepodge of subject matter. The "open door" policy toward learning could mean that the student would spend all of his time learning the trite and the insignificant.

A more serious weakness of the coherence theory is that of defeatism. If we accept the assumption that the truth in its entirety is infinite and therefore unknowable and that man's chief purpose is to seek this complete truth, then man is defeated before he starts. One may well question any set of assumptions which holds so little promise of a sense of fulfillment.

Summary and Terminology

As you have read through the foregoing sections, you have probably been aware of the relationship of these various theories of truth to the theories of man discussed in the preceding chapter. Indeed, we have not launched out in a new subject but are looking again at our central subject—the curriculum. Each of the theories of truth discussed here has its parallel in the theories of the nature of the learner.

The warning which was given earlier must be repeated. We should not be led into the trap of thinking that each of these views about the subject matter automatically leads to a certain kind of curriculum content. It is not so simple as that. There are many combinations of philosophies possible, and most philosophers—as well as most practitioners—may combine and modify the assumptions from several schools of thought. Each of us is to some degree an eclectic. Philosophers, too, tend to resist pat conclusions as to theories and their implications.

The correspondence theory of truth is to be associated with the theory of natural evil. Notice how the two fit together. If we assume that man has a natural predisposition toward evil, then he must look outside of himself for the source of good. To find the source of good and truth, one must look to some ultimate and absolute truth. Thus the correspondence theory with its emphasis on such truth goes with the theory of natural evil under the educational doctrine of *Authoritarianism* or *Essentialism*.

The intuitive theory of truth belongs with the theory of natural good. The view that man is born with a natural predisposition toward good leads logically to his being the source of truth. The individual is thus raised to a position of prominence because of his inborn awareness of truth and his inborn goodness. The doctrine of *Idealism* presented in the previous chapter represents this set of philosophic assumptions.

The pragmatic theory of truth, being one aspect of pragmatism or experimentalism, finds its counterpart in the theory of evolving man. As man struggles to master his own experiences, he needs no absolute or universal sense of truth. He needs only to find the truth of his own experiences to have a guide for courageous and purposeful living. The educational philosophy we have labeled *Pragmatism* is based on these fundamental assumptions.

And finally the coherence theory of truth is a fitting partner to the theory of the aspiring man. Man, being a seeking creature, looks all about himself to find truth. And he can find it, for the truth is everywhere to be found. His aspiration to find more and more truth is thus fulfilled by its availability. Granted that the truth can never be found in its entirety, still it is in the quest for it that man can find his greatest happiness and sense of accomplishment. These assumptions are basic to the educational philosophy called *Realism*. We have encountered the term in the previous chapter; we will encounter it again later.

One should not conclude that these four are the only theories of truth held by philosophers. There are others, but these four are the representatives of contemporary educational thought and therefore have been discussed in detail.

At the beginning of this chapter we saw how the selection of subject matter for learning experiences is usually made according to such practical considerations as authoritative opinion, the felt needs of the child, adult needs, or needs for further learning. Rarely is attention given to such philosophic considerations as are discussed in this chapter. Yet a careful view of these practical reasons show that they are actually outgrowths of the theories of truth which we have considered.

If one bases the selection of subject matter on the authoritative opinion of the textbook or state course of study, he is following the correspondence theory of truth and authoritarianism. If the students' felt needs are the teacher's prime concern, he is adopting the Idealistic philosophy and the intuitive theory of truth. The use of the adult needs criterion belongs to the Pragmatic theory; and subject matter selection based on its contribution to future learning is actually the result of assumptions of the Realistic philosophy and the coherence theory of truth. These are usually applications which are made without our being aware of the theories which lie behind our action. Nevertheless, our choices must be made in terms of some assumptions which are basic to the philosophies studied. To make decisions as to the content of the curriculum for any school program is no easy matter. The sounder our assumptions as to the nature of truth, the better our decisions will be.

CHAPTER IV

•

THE LEARNING PROCESS

In the last two chapters we have examined the most obvious elements of the curriculum, the learner and the subject matter. We come now to a less obvious but equally vital ingredient of the curriculum, the process whereby the former two are brought into conjunction so that learning takes place. Unless this happens—unless the subject matter is absorbed by the learner and made a part of his total being—these two components may just as well exist oceans apart.

And yet it does happen. Learning does occur. And when ones sees it happen, when one knows it has happened to him, one can but stand in awe of the event. Small wonder that one psychologist titled an article relating to the subject, "The Miracle of Learning."[1] For a miracle it is—as great a miracle as the biblical parting of the waters of the Red Sea or the changing of water into wine.

Our examination of the learning process differs significantly in one way from our study of either the learner or the subject matter. It is here that we find the closest relationship between philosophy and psychology. This relationship which was discussed in Chapter One is fundamental to our discussion of the learning process; for it is from psychology that we have gained most of our insights into how learning takes place. But psychology has not found final answers to the nature and conditions of learning. It remains the task of philosophy to develop and examine assumptions which explain the findings of psychological research.

---

[1] James L. Mursell, "The Miracle of Learning," *Atlantic*, June, 1935, pp. 733-741.

The Learning Process

If we examine the learning process, certain facts about it come into clear perspective. We must begin with an exterior force or object which has the potential of being learned from. This we can call the *stimulus object*. It may take the form of a printed page, a picture, a microscope slide, a view of the ocean, the sound of a violin, the sight of a flower, or any of the millions of other environmental phenomena which have the potential of being learned or learned from. These stimulus objects must be capable of producing some form of energy. The violin string's vibration produces sound waves; the flower reflects light rays. It is this *stimulus energy* which impinges upon the organism by way of the sense organs. Each sense organ, or receptor, has the same basic function; it converts the stimulus energy into nerve impulses. The retina of the eye converts light into the electro-chemical energy of the nervous system; the cochlea of the ear converts sound waves into nerve energy; etc. This step of learning, which we will call *internalization* or *sensation,* consists of getting that which exists outside the body into the nervous system.

But all nerve impulses are basically the same; one can sense no difference between an impulse originating in the eye and one which rises in the ear or the finger tips. Somehow, when these impulses reach the brain they must be unscrambled —each must find its own meaning within the individual. This occurs partially as a result of certain brain areas serving as receiving stations for nerve impulses from certain sense organs. But beyond this, there is a process which as yet we are unable to explain whereby new nerve impulses are associated with similar ones received from previous experience. The new experience comes to have meaning to the learner in terms of his past experience. This process is called *perception*.

In order for the learning to be complete, a final step must be made; it must be given permanence. In this step, called *integration,* the things which are learned become a part of the personality structure of the learner. We see, hear, smell, feel, and otherwise experience thousands of things every day of our lives. Only a fraction of these become a permanent deposit in our bank of learnings. This selection of some things and casting off of others represents the final stage of the learning process.

With this selection the learning process can be said to be completed.

Having so analyzed the learning process, we come to the realization that we have not said what actually happens; we have described learning, we have not explained it. The great question remains, "How does learning occur?" For in spite of our most valiant efforts to explore the process of learning it still defies a complete and comprehensive explanation. The miracle of learning is also the mystery of learning.

EARLY EFFORTS TO EXPLAIN LEARNING

The mystery of learning must have been as much of a dilemma to early man as it is to us today. Primitive man, in spite of the limitations of his tools and techniques to accomplish his tasks, was nevertheless a thinking, rational creature. He too tried to find answers even though his limited cultural heritage caused his answers to be of a superstitious nature. Awed by the mysteries of his world, he found it possible to couch his answers only in terms of mystery. So it was with his early efforts to explain learning; he had to satisfy himself by use of a magical formula which referred to external forces such as good and evil spirits or the journey work of stars.

As man grew more sophisticated, his explanations began to be more complex and systematic. One of the most common of these more advanced explanations was that of divine revelation, which we examined as one concept of truth in Chapter Three. Seen as a view of learning, this theory stated that all of man's knowledge was the gift of the gods. Although it served the purpose of telling what the source of all knowledge is, it did not explain learning and was thus little better than a meaningless generality.

The philosophers of ancient Greece carried these concepts still further. No theory of learning is more fascinating than that of Plato (427?–347 B.C.). He saw existence as being of two levels. The first level is composed of the real, true, and perfect world as it exists in "nature." (Plato's "nature" is somewhat elusive to us who have been schooled in more scientific thought, but it may be defined as *God* or *perfection* in modern lan-

64

guage.) The second level consists of the world as *perceived* by
man with all of its imperfections and errors. Man can never
know the world of nature directly, he can only know a shadowy
projection of that world as it is reflected from the perfect world.

But man, Plato said, is himself a product of nature; he
comes into this world as a creation of God. He is thus a product of the perfect world and therefore, at one time—before his
birth—knew all things in their perfect form. But something
happens when we are born. The perfect knowledge we had is
lost. Our birth is but a forgetting of things we once knew in
perfection. This forgetting is not a complete loss, however, for
a ghost of what was once known is retained.

As we have experiences throughout life, reasoned Plato,
these ghosts are revived; our learnings are actually rediscoveries
of that which lies, half hidden, in our memories. We can thus
be led to the discovery of truth already known to us if our
teachers are wise enough to guide us toward this discovery.
Although we can never know the perfect world of nature as
we once knew it, we can be led to an ever increasing recognition of the perceived world as a reflection of that perfect world.
This Platonic belief is referred to as *the doctrine of innate ideas.*

Such concepts as learning by divine revelation and the doctrine of innate ideas held sway for many years. They were
strengthened by the religious ideas of the time, for through
these ideas there could be established a relationship between
God and man that bespoke of the power of God and the capacity of man to receive divine inspiration.

In the seventeenth century, a new philosophy rose to challenge these earlier concepts. Called *empiricism,* this view of
learning proposed the fundamental assumption that man's only
way of learning is through experience. This concept may seem
trite to us today; most of us have heard little else. At the time
it was declared, however, it was regarded as a revolutionary
concept, for it cut loose from the religious thinking of the day
by placing man's experience rather than his relationship to God
at the center point of the learning process. Although there
were several contributors to the doctrine of empiricism, it was
the English philosopher John Locke (1632–1704) who did the

most to make a formal statement of the philosophy. His efforts were to have a lasting effect upon the school curriculum.

Locke compared the mind of the child at birth to a blank slate, a *tabula rasa*. Each experience is as though our slates are being written on; and the total of such writings represents the total learning of the person during his lifetime. He carried his analogy further by explaining individual differences in capacity in terms of the "hardness" of the slate. Some slates are easily etched upon, thus more is gained from experience with less effort; others are hard and resistant to etching, thus making learning more difficult.

The emergence of empiricism laid the foundation from which a science of psychology could develop. Philosophers such as David Hume, James Mill, Johann Herbart, and Gottfried Leibnitz in the eighteenth and early nineteenth centuries accepted the new concept of learning; and Johannes Müller, E. H. Webber, and Gustav Fechner accepted empiricism as the basis of their experiments in psycho-physics.

From these beginnings, Wilhelm Wundt (1832–1920) took inspiration and in 1879 opened the first psychological institute at the University of Leipzig. This date has come to be regarded as the birth year of modern scientific psychology, and Wundt is sometimes referred to as the "father of experimental psychology." Obviously, no revolution in method or thought occurs with a ringing proclamation. But in the case of Wundt's institute the ideas, the methods of study, and the general intellectual atmosphere *did* change the world of psychology.

The chief change was to move psychology from the realm of armchair theorizing into the laboratory. Psychology became a science; and the methods, attitudes, and outlook which were promulgated were those which reflected an experimental viewpoint rather than a deductive system. The basic assumption which was evidenced in the work of Wundt and his followers was that human behavior is orderly and predictable and is therefore subject to scientific study. Human behavior was regarded as being governed by principles and laws just as is every other phenomenon of the universe. Psychologists since the time of Wundt have been committed to the task of determining what those principles and laws are. By such a commitment the foundations have been laid for the scientific study of learning.

The outstanding theory of learning to emerge in the late nineteenth century has been given the name *faculty psychology.* For its point of origin it went back to the ancient Greeks and the writings of Aristotle (384–322 B.C.). Aristotle saw the psyche (or soul) of man as being composed of five factors or faculties. These were: the nutritive faculty (the ability of the organism to maintain itself); the desiring faculty; the perceptual faculty (including aesthetic sensitivity); the locomotive faculty; and thinking power. Aristotle believed the objective of education to be the development of these faculties in such a manner that they could function with the greatest effectiveness possible.[2]

It was John Locke who took these rudimentary ideas of Aristotle and developed them into a comprehensive theory of the learning process. Locke maintained that the processes of mind (memory, logic, introspection, and the like) are capable of being developed and perfected through learning. This is to say a child can be taught memory, or logic and reasoning, or any other mental process. Locke maintained that "as the strength of the body lies chiefly in being able to endure hardships, so also does that of the mind."[3]

Locke's statements led to a means of applying the theory to classroom practice. Called *mental discipline,* the practice advocated was that of strengthening the faculties by exercising them. In the same way a muscle is made more efficient by exercise, a faculty is strengthened through use. Further, as we strengthen each of these faculties, the overall strength of the mind increases and we become more intelligent. Mental discipline, then, promulgated the belief that native ability is improved through rigorous exercise of the faculties that compose it.

---

[2] W. D. Ross (ed.), *Aristotle: Selections* (New York: Scribners, 1955), Sec. 62-68.

[3] Peter Gay (ed.), *John Locke on Education* (New York: Bureau of Publications, Teachers College, Columbia University, 1964), p. 26.

During the eighteenth and nineteenth centuries the theory of faculty psychology was further developed and by 1900 had grown in both its import and its comprehensiveness. Psychologists and philosophers made attempts to define and classify the various faculties. In a psychology book published in 1886 this statement was made as an ultimate truth about all learning:

> The great law underlying the processes of development is that the faculties or functions of the intellect are strengthened by exercise. Thus the power of observation improves by the repeated exercise of the power.[4]

The same book contained a listing of the various faculties with a discussion as to how each could be exercised most effectively. The listing included these eleven faculties: attention, sense discrimination, observation, memory, imagination, generalization, judgment, feeling, higher sentiments (morality, ethics, etc.), will, and character.

The acceptance of this theory by schoolmen led to curriculum programs which incorporated the practices of mental discipline. Indeed, it may be argued that no single set of assumptions have had a more telling effect on the school curriculum than have those of the theory of faculty psychology and the resulting practices of mental discipline.

If the faculties could be improved by practice, those who accepted this theory argued, then the inclusion of certain types of experiences and activities in the school program could be advocated or justified in terms of their value as a "discipline." Geometry was to be included in the curriculum on the grounds that the study of it increased the individual's logic and reasoning power, while the memorization of the vocabulary of a foreign language would increase the individual's ability to remember names, or dates, or telephone numbers. Even the practical arts were justified in these terms; mechanical drawing was believed to increase neatness, and woodworking developed a desire in the individual for habits of industry and careful workmanship.

About the turn of the twentieth century, however, a num-

---

[4]James Sully, *Teacher's Handbook of Psychology* (New York: Appleton, 1886), p. 49.

The Learning Process

ber of attacks were made on faculty psychology. Philosophers and psychologists began to question not only whether the theory was an adequate explanation of learning, but also whether the claims made for it were valid. Psychologists such as William James (1842–1910) put the contentions of mental discipline to the test of experimental research and found that they simply did not stand up under the scrutiny of such research. Children who spent long hours in the learning of poems could not memorize a new poem any better than those who had not strengthened their memory faculty, and students who studied geometry were no more logical or rational in areas other than geometry than those who had not had such a course. The pin of research had burst the balloon of faculty psychology.

Dissatisfaction with faculty psychology was also expressed on philosophic grounds. There is a unity underlying all learning which is ignored by faculty psychology, said those who disagreed with the theory. Why is it that certain physical activity brings into being streams of thoughts and ideas? Why do habits developed in one area actually impede learning in other areas? For instance, the study of two foreign languages at the same time may cause confusion if the languages are of different origins. This lack of unity in the theory of faculty psychology was also considered by them reason to distrust it.

TRANSFER

But if the theory of faculty psychology was invalid, how could our curriculum practices be justified? If there is no improvement in a faculty by practice, this would imply that each item must be learned separately and without regard to any other learning. And yet we know this is not the case. The learning of Latin vocabulary does not improve one's memory but it does improve one's English vocabulary. It became necessary to reexamine the learning process and to attempt to find some further explanation that would be both valid and practical in its implication.

In this quest for a new explanation of the learning process, psychologists hit upon *transfer* as a valid and usable explanation. Simply put, transfer is the use of something gained in one learning experience in a new and different experience.

In a classic experiment, Charles H. Judd (1873–1946) had two groups of children throw darts at a target submerged in twelve inches of water. One group was then taught about light refraction, but no connection was made between this and its dart throwing. The two groups did equally well in learning to hit the target by trial and error when it was at the twelve-inch level. When the depth of the target was changed to three inches, however, the group that had studied about light refraction was able to adapt to the new situation while the other group had to begin a new trial and error process. The conclusion was drawn that the children had transferred their knowledge of light refraction to the dart throwing activity.

From this experiment Judd arrived at the conclusion that transfer was the result of generalization. By this he meant that we are able to use something learned in one situation in another situation if we are capable of discerning what principles are involved. Thus the students who knew the principle of light refraction were able to transfer this knowledge to dart throwing at a submerged target.

E. L. Thorndike (1874–1949) took issue with Judd on his explanation of transfer and developed his own theory to explain the phenomenon, called the *theory of identical elements*. Thorndike's contention was that we can recognize similar factors in two situations or experiences. The study of Latin aids in the development of vocabulary only of those English words of Latin derivation; it is useless in the mastery of Anglo-Saxon words, for there are no common elements in the vocabulary of the two languages. Transfer, then, he said, can be practiced only to the extent that the two situations have parts or elements which are the same in both.

Still another concept has emerged in recent years which explains transfer in terms of the structuring or organizing of learning experiences. This view, called *transfer by transposition*, holds that the similarity between experiences lies in the relationship of the internal structure of the parts rather than similarity of the parts themselves. We are able to transfer to the extent that we can recognize this likeness in structure. For example, "America the Beautiful" played in the key of C is recognizable even though the individual has never heard it played in that key. From this can be inferred that the perception of the music is in terms of the relationship of the notes composing the melody rather than in terms of the notes themselves.

The various research evidences and explanations of transfer have done much to shape our ideas about the value of certain types of experiences in the curriculum. One of our chief criteria in the selection of instructional practices has become that of the potential transfer value.

Some confusion exists when one compares transfer with its predecessor, faculty psychology. Indeed, some educators insist that we have only kicked faculty psychology out of the back door in order to invite it in the front door with a new name. Therefore a comparison of the two would probably be wise.

Faculty psychology puts its emphasis on the development of qualities or characteristics which will find their way into other activities—thus neatness, reasoning, memory, etc., which are practiced in one situation become a characteristic of the learner which may be used in a different situation. Transfer, however, refers to a learning outcome—such as knowledge, understanding, or skills which are the same as required in the new situation and are applied there. Advocates of faculty psychology assume that the use of the improved faculty occurs automatically within any area where it has application. Thus the improvement of memory affects all memory work. Transfer, however, is not assumed by its advocates to occur automatically; it may not happen at all unless the student recognizes the similarities in the two situations. Although some brighter people may be more able in discovering transfer potential than others, they continue, in many cases there is a need for the student to be taught how to transfer. Thus, while faculty psychology holds that the improved faculty influences other behavior automatically, transfer is not deemed to occur without a purposeful effort to transfer.

ASSOCIATIONAL THEORIES

The late nineteenth and early twentieth centuries have brought forth a number of new theories which attempt to dig deeper into the nature and causes of learning. Called the *associational theories* (for reasons we shall see later), these theories were developed out of an attempt to be more scientific in the study of learning theory.

Early in the twentieth century E. L. Thorndike began a series of animal experiments which eventually resulted in a theory of learning destined to have great effect on the curriculum of American schools. Called *connectionism,* the theory advanced was the most comprehensive yet to be developed.

Thorndike reasoned that all behavior had its parallel in the nervous system of the organism; each new learning represented a modification in the function of the nervous system. To Thorndike, the cerebral cortex is like a huge telephone or electrical switchboard with an infinite number of connections possible. When a new fact, idea, or skill is learned, there must be a change in the neural paths or connections in the cerebral cortex—thus the name connectionism. Each time we practice a response which is successful in meeting our needs we entrench or make more binding the connection. Learning can thus be defined as the building of neural bonds between stimuli and responses.

On the basis of his research, Thorndike created a number of principles which govern the effectiveness of the learning experience. Chief among these are his *three laws of learning*—readiness, exercise, and effect. Readiness implies a set to learn, a preparedness of a neurological circuit to perform its function. If the organism is ready to learn, the response pattern will produce satisfaction and a tendency to repeat the response. If the organism is not ready, even if the response is forced, the activity will produce only annoyance and a tendency to avoid repeating the response. Exercise refers to repetition of a stimulus-response pattern. The more a learning is repeated, the more the neurological connection is "stamped in" and the more readily will the desired response result. Effect refers to the feeling which results from the learning. We tend to repeat those activities which are satisfying to us and to discontinue those which produce pain or unpleasantness. The effect of learning may be the result of the same internal feelings of satisfaction described in the law of readiness. They may also be, however, the results of rewards or punishments presented by the teacher.

Forgetting is explained by Thorndike as the result of disuse. When neural connections are not used, they tend to fade. Thus you may be unable to read a Latin prose passage in spite of having once been competent in the language. Since you have not used this ability, the neural passages which compose it have faded.

Later in his life Thorndike modified his views on several of these principles, but his basic view of learning remained the same.

Another associational theory to gain prominence was originated by John B. Watson (1878–1958) and is called *behaviorism*. Although it holds much in common with Thorndike's connectionism, there are radical differences in some of its basic assumptions which result in different curriculum practices.

The most radical of these differences is in the view of psychology itself as a field of study. Watson insisted that psychology must concern itself only with the things which can be studied scientifically. Thoughts and feelings, Watson stated, are internal and can be examined only through introspection, and inasmuch as there is no way to validate the findings of introspection, such study is non-scientific and should be discarded. What can be studied, he said, is the organism's overt behavior (thus the name behaviorism), for it alone can be observed, measured, and validated by an "outsider." He renounced all theories which attempted to explain learning in terms of internal modification; only the change of overt behavior could be regarded as learning.

In his effort to find an explanation for learning, Watson went back to the work of the Russian physiologist Ivan Pavlov (1849–1936). It was Pavlov who had discovered experimental evidence of the conditioned response in dogs. Watson surmised that virtually all learning comes about through a similar conditioning process. Therefore, he thought that a child could be taught any desired reaction by simply arranging stimuli so that certain responses would be produced.

Watson's theory is unique in several ways. As was pointed out, it views learning only in terms of behavior itself rather than in terms of any physiological or neurological construct. It also ignores such factors as native ability, interest, or readiness. Watson argued that any child could be taught anything if the conditions were right.

Watson's theory is less comprehensive than Thorndike's, but it does have the strength of being more scientific. The passage of the years has seen an increasing amount of laboratory research which has validated, elaborated, and further developed it.

The connectionism of Thorndike and the behaviorism of Watson have, as you might expect, been modified and elaborated by disciples of these pioneers. There are differences in the two theories in their basic assumptions. There are, however, in all associational learning theories certain common assumptions or principles which underlie them.

The first and most obvious of these common characteristics is their *atomistic* view of learning. This is to say that each learning is a separate and distinct entity. The child must learn each thing as an item unto itself (e.g., each addition combination must be memorized separately). Learning so viewed becomes an accumulative affair with each learning being added to a stockpile of previously learned material. This is not to deny the existence of transfer; but each transference is in itself a separate and distinct learning item. Associational theories are often referred to as *S-R bond theories* because each stimulus is believed to produce its own reaction. This atomistic nature is to be found not only in the material being learned but also in the learning processes themselves.

A second major assumption in all associational theory is that learning involves the internalizing of material. The role of the environment is of vast importance because it provides the original impetus for learning to occur, and the chief products of learning reside within the learner. In short, learning is an outside-to-inside affair.

Another common assumption about learning held by all associational theorists is implied in the name of the theory itself; all of their viewpoints emphasize the role of the association of ideas. They would say that as new things are learned, they are classified or associated with things which have already been mastered. Each new experience is perceived, learned, and retained as a separate entity; it does not exist independently but always in association or conjunction with previous learning. According to them, when the child learns to read the word "dog," he learns it as an individual word, but the word stirs up all of the mental images, memories, and concepts he has developed about dogs. The word when read brings into being a flood of "flashbacks" which are associated with the new learning and thus give meaning to it.

It should also be noted that associational theories are uniform in giving importance to repetition as a requisite to learning. Thorndike's law of exercise is illustrative of this point as is Watson's view that repetition acts as a reinforcement in the conditioning process. All associational theories look upon repetition, drill, and practice as a key to successful learning.

The curriculum implications of associational theories are easy to discern. If a curriculum is based on such a view of learning, it will be marked by a progress of learning through small units of material. Words will be learned singularly without regard to context as will mathematical processes and the facts of history. It is the contention of these theories that by learning enough of these isolated facts the student will be able to associate them with each other and with past learning so that he will have the basis for transferring learning to new situations.

In a classroom dominated by associational theory, we would also observe an abundance of the use of drill as a method of teaching. Whether justified on the basis of Thorndike's law of exercise or on the building of conditioned responses as advocated by Watson, the curriculum practice would be the same—the use of repetition and practice as a way of learning.

Attention would be paid in such a classroom to motivation. But this motivation would not necessarily be of an intrinsic nature such as interest in the subject by the student. It could just as well be extrinsic rewards such as grades, the teacher's approval, or gold stars acting as motivating factors. According to this theory, any behavior can be reinforced, and rewards for learning act as reinforcement.

Finally, curriculum construction in the associational view is an easy process. Inasmuch as learning is accomplished by the accumulation of small bits of knowledge, the curriculum can be viewed as but the total of such bits. The content of the curriculum can be built by determining which learnings are to be sought and then setting about to teach these learnings.

GENETIC PSYCHOLOGY

Genetic psychology is the name given to another view of the learning process which begins with an entirely different set of assumptions. Whereas the theories we have studied to this point emphasized the internalizing of experience resulting from environmental forces, genetic psychology views learning as an internal process involving the growth and development of the individual's personality.

The foundations of this theory go all the way back to Plato and his doctrine of innate ideas. The concept that the child at one time knew perfection and has subsequently forgotten it in the birth process implies that the child is actually relearning when he goes through learning experiences. The learning process, then, becomes one of the internal development of that which is already there rather than the presentation of new materials from outside the learner. The underlying assumption of this theory is that the learning process is one of internal development, and this assumption is fundamental to all genetic views.

In more recent times the writings and educational practices of Friedrich Froebel (1782–1852) served to develop the concept of genetic psychology further. Froebel viewed learning as a matter of revelation through nature. He saw in the universe an orderly, unified system, and he believed this system to be the result of powerful, mystical forces. It would follow that this unity extends to the child himself inasmuch as he is a part of nature. Therefore, according to Froebel, there is a mystical union between the child and his natural world which is to be discovered rather than taught to the child as new information. Through his play activities, his free association with other children, and his experimenting with his environment, he will develop ideas and concepts which are consistent with the universals of nature. Through handling a ring, for example, the child can learn of eternity; through building with blocks he can learn of the order of the universe.

The Learning Process

From Sigmund Freud the genetic view of learning received further, though incidental, support. Freud's view of the personality was a developmental theory; that is, he saw personality as a continually growing thing. The individual, Freud said, can only be understood in terms of the entire course of his life—the joys, pains, frustrations, and achievements that have brought him to his present being. He saw the early years as crucial in the shaping of the personality. Learning, he said, is more than the accumulation of knowledge; it is the means whereby the individual becomes a person. If the child learns self-acceptance and the willingness to deal with his problems at the conscious level, he will develop into a happy, well-adjusted person; if he learns to repress his feelings, his hostilities, and his guilt, he will suffer emotional disturbances or personality dissociation. Viewed in these terms, learning becomes synonymous with personality development.

An American educator, G. Stanley Hall (1846–1924), became one of the chief spokesmen for genetic psychology at the turn of the century. He also did much to formulate the belief into a logical, systematic, and comprehensive theory of learning. Hall had approached the study of psychology through biological channels and became convinced that the recapitulation theory (that the biological development of each individual repeats the biological history of the race) was not only applicable to physiological growth but also to the social and educational development of the child. The child, said Hall, goes through stages of development and learning which are like those reflected by man in his entire history; he is at one stage a hunter, at another, a builder, etc. Therefore in teaching the child, the experiences which we plan for him must follow this sequence of development. The purpose of education, according to Hall, is to guide the evolution of the child's personality to the highest possible level of development.

In Italy, Maria Montessori (1870–1952) began to develop a curriculum which was a reflection of genetic psychology's explanation of learning. Although Montessori did not embrace any particular view of learning proposed by earlier thinkers, she developed a method for instruction of young children which emphasized the development of learning through individual

77

activities. Several characteristics of the method are particularly noteworthy. It involves maximum freedom for the child to experiment and discover for himself instead of being told which responses are correct; it encourages cooperation among the students; it is well suited to care for individual differences inasmuch as each child progresses at his own rate; and it stresses the role of learning through the senses by having the child work with specially prepared materials suited to his developmental level. Although it should be emphasized that Montessori was more of a practitioner than a philosopher, she did create a method of teaching which carried out in detail the curriculum implications of genetic psychology.

In recent years there have been other writers and thinkers who have made further contributions to the view of learning as developmental activity rather than as the internalization of environmental stimuli.

One of the more outstanding of these contemporary writers is Robert J. Havighurst (1900–), whose concept of "developmental tasks" is an attempt to explain learning in terms of a sequence of essential experiences resulting from the needs of children at varying stages of development. To Havighurst, learning is not a matter of compiling factual knowledge; it is a process of growth in which each age level presents the child with challenges, some of which are of internal origin, others of which come about by virtue of his living in a certain social scheme. As each challenge is presented the child must come to grips with it, learn how to cope with it, and learn the skills, understandings, and attitudes required to progress through it. If he succeeds in meeting the challenge, he will progress to his next level of development where he will be faced with new developmental tasks which are pertinent to that level. If he fails, he will be ill-equipped for the new challenges he must face and will suffer a good deal of unhappiness thereby. If the failure is great enough, it can result in an immature adult with fixations related to his earlier growth failures, or with neurotic or psychotic tendencies.

Anthropologists such as Ashley Montagu (1905–) have given still further credence to the assumptions of genetic psychology. Through his study of primitive peoples, Montagu has come to the conclusion that it is through learning that the individual becomes a human being. From simple, direct experiences growing out of his basic needs, the individual evolves toward more complex, subtle, and humanlike experiences which make him a fit member of human society.

No single person more etpitomizes the present state of genetic psychology than does Jean Piaget (1896–), who has attracted international attention in his work and writings at Rousseau Institute in Geneva, Switzerland. It is impossible to do justice to the many contributions of this giant in the field of educational psychology in a few sentences; he is a voluminous writer and in the last forty years has probably contributed more ideas than any single writer in the field of genetic psychology. We can, however, list his main tenets even though we must do so in shorthand.

Piaget has taken a strong stand against the concept that learning is a stockpiling of ideas. He insists that learning can only be viewed as changed behavior. His statement, "I only know to the extent that I can act," is typical of his view of learning.

Piaget has also given a good deal of attention to concept formation according to the level of development of the learner. According to him, young children form concepts in terms of themselves and their own activities. The four-year-old may think that the sun "goes to bed" when it goes down, but as the child develops he begins to lose this egocentric view of the world and creates more embracing concepts. He will, during later childhood, form concepts which center in his physical or material world and still later beome capable of abstractions.

Piaget has also given language a prominent place in this evolution of concepts. To him language is more than a communication of ideas—language is the principal tool of thought. To the extent the child is able to verbalize his experiences and concepts, he can build a consistent, internal structure of these ideas.

To summarize, Piaget sees concept formation as the end product of all learning, and these concepts are but a part of the growth and development of the child.

It should also be noted that in the United States we have

seen a revival of the methods of Montessori in the last decade. Particularly in parochial elementary schools there has been increasing attention given to the materials and methods which aim at the development of the child through the education of his senses in a stimulating environment.

What are the common elements of all genetic psychology? What are the curriculum practices which come into being if one adopts this view of learning? As with the other theories we have discussed, if we accept the assumptions of genetic psychology, we can draw conclusions as to the nature of the curriculum which reflects its postulates.

There would be, for instance, a great deal of emphasis given to the placement of experiences according to the level of the child's development. Great care would be taken to see that learning advances from step to step in an evolutionary process matching the growth pace of the child.

But this pacing of experience would not be for the purpose of assuring that the child masters content. It would be because the objective of learning is growth and development of the personality. Growth, development, adjustment, and learning are all synonymous terms in the genetic view.

All genetic psychology emphasizes the role of freedom of learning. If the child is hemmed in by too many rules and regulations, it will inhibit his experimenting and discovering. He will be unable to develop as he should; his learning and thus his personality will be stifled or thwarted.

Genetic psychologists also give credence to the individuality of learning. Each child must grow at his own pace and in his own way. The curriculum cannot be preset but must be continually evolving. It must keep pace with the growth needs of each individual. They would say that, in a very real sense, it is wrong to speak of *the* curriculum, for each child has his own curriculum.

FIELD THEORIES

John Amos Comenius (1592–1670), a Moravian bishop and a leading educational theorist of his time, did much to open the door to still another view of learning, the *field theory*. Comenius insisted that learning came into being as a result of perception of the world through the senses rather than entirely as the result of intellectual effort. Comenius was therefore interested in the way the child perceives his environment rather than the association of ideas resulting from this perception. Comenius was the first educator to develop a theory of learning which emphasized the senses and the organization of stimuli.

It was not until the twentieth century that new theories came into existence which elaborated this view. The new concepts became variously known as field theory, gestalt psychology, holistic, or organismic psychology. The German psychologist Max Wertheimer (1880–1943) was the first to create a systematic psychological theory which attempted to explain learning in more comprehensive terms than did the associational theorists. Wertheimer was primarily interested in perception, and through his experiments arrived at the conclusion that we perceive our environmental stimuli as whole units rather than as individual items. He maintained that the traditional S-R bond was totally unrealistic, because the S of the formula involves the totality of perceived environment rather than the individual items. Further, said Wertheimer, this whole environment is not simply the total of stimuli—it has an existence of its own which results from the interrelationships of its parts. The whole is greater than the sum of its parts. As we perceive our world, we may "fill in" parts which are not present or we may react to situations as though they were complete even though we receive only partial cues. We do so, he said, because we perceive the total in terms of patterns, configurations, or structures.

Wolfgang Koehler (1887–   ) added much to the field theory with his study of the learning behavior of chimpanzees. In an attempt to discover how such animals perform learning tasks, he presented them with problematic situations and observed their behavior. In his most famous experiment he put chimpanzees into a cage in which they had to put together two sections of a pole in order to reach their food. Although this problem lay beyond the comprehension of some of the chimpanzees, some were able to solve the problem. The peculiarities of the learning lay in the fact that these chimpanzees solved the problem without resorting to trial and error. They seemed to suddenly grasp what was required of them, and once having solved the problem they did not forget the solution or hesitate in getting their food. Nor did drill nor practice seem to play any part in this learning; the chimpanzee's first success was a complete and finished learning task.

On the basis of this evidence Koehler reasoned that something in learning occurred which could not be explained by associational theories. He concluded that learning is a total rather than a fragmentary process and this total process could be called *insightful learning.*

Perhaps none of the learning concepts of field theory carries more force than does this concept of learning as the product of insight. According to this concept, the phenomenon of learning is characterized by a sudden complete discovery of the principle or generality which is the key to the problem one is facing. Thus Archimedes' discovery of the principle of density of solids as he sat in his bathtub would be a perfect example of the attainment of insight. Although the ordinary learner has little hope of developing insight as significant as that of Archimedes, each of us can achieve it at lesser levels. When the child discovers the principle of multiplication of numbers, or when the student of a foreign language ceases to translate and becomes capable of thinking in that language, he is experiencing insightful learning.

The concept of *the field* is of prime importance in understanding how the individual perceives objects and events. According to Wertheimer, we perceive objects and events in terms of total patterns or gestalts. Stimuli always occur in context, and responses are total responses to this perceived field. Advancing this concept further, he surmised that the entire personality structure and the totality of experiences go together in an interactional relationship. This perception, response, and interactional relationship constitute what has been variously called the "life space," the "gestalt," or simply "the field." But regardless of the name, this concept holds that all things derive their meaning from the thing of which they are a part. The field is not an environmental structure, however, but exists as a perceived entity within the learner.

Another peculiarity of field theories of learning involves

the global nature or the underlying unity of learning. Insight is identifiable as being a *total* process. Paralleling this totality of learning is a unity which exists in the very nature of ideas and concepts. The structure and organization of insight is as important as the content of these insights. It is this unity that makes possible the grasping of large, comprehensive concepts, and these concepts are the most transferable and most lasting of all learnings. Without this unity, learning would be nothing but the compilation of trivia.

A German psychologist, Kurt Lewin (1890–1947), who immigated to the United States at the time of Hitler's rise to power became the chief disciple of field theory in this country. He enlarged the theory to make it more than an explanation of learning; he made it a theory of personality as well. To Lewin learning theory and personality theory were inseparable for it is through learning that the structure of the self, the perception of the environment, and the interrelationships of these two factors are developed. To him, the total of these forces constitutes the *life space* of the individual. It is this life space which determines the organization and content of the personality.

Lewin also enlarged our ideas of the learning environment by showing that the emotional atmosphere of the classroom influences the activities and learning which occur therein. In experiments which have become classic, he demonstrated that the type of leadership provided by the teacher—autocratic, democratic, or laissez faire—influenced the behavior of the children. He thus demonstrated that the field of learning involves the entire situation in which the individual exists.

The followers of John Dewey (1859–1952) found inspiration for their cause in the field theory. The emphasis on problem solving as the method of learning is a common element in both field theory and Dewey's philosophy. Dewey was concerned with the use or utility value of learning. He developed the concept that the value of all ideas, thoughts, and feelings lies in their usefulness in solving the problems which men face in day-to-day living. Dewey called his contention *instrumentalism,* for he saw learning as an active instrument to be applied in the solution of problems rather than as a compilation of facts, understandings, and habits. In his analysis of the problematic situation Dewey showed how the learner who finds himself facing a problem sets up tentative hypotheses and selects from these hypotheses the one which seems most plausible and proceeds to act upon it. It is through this creation and testing of hypotheses, he said, that concepts are formed. He saw conceptualization as a practical matter growing out of the individual's needs.

The curriculum implications for field theories of learning are as unique as those for the other schools of thought we have described. Chief among these would be the organization of learning experiences into comprehensive blocks or units. The evolution of unit teaching as a curriculum device is a direct result of adopting field theory in curriculum constrution.

Another curriculum implication in field theory is its emphasis on conceptual learning. In a school in which field theory is applied to curriculum construction, the experiences would be planned so as to insure the development of large comprehensive ideas rather than the accumulation of isolated bits of knowledge.

This emphasis on conceptual learning has been responsible for some of the major curricular innovations of the last two decades. We have seen the development of curriculum projects, particularly in the areas of science and mathematics, which are aimed toward conceptualization rather than toward the accumulation of facts. Typical of these projects are those of the Biological Survey Curriculum Study, the Physical Science Study Commission, and the Science and Mathematics Study Group.

In keeping with this objective of concept development, there would be a minimum of drill in such a curriculum. According to this view, inasmuch as the repetition of the bits of information is unnecessary to the development of insight, there is little if anything to be gained through such practices.

Finally, since the insight which field theorists regard as the ultimate in learning is most likely to come into being through problem solving, a curriculum founded on this theory would emphasize that type of activity in the classroom. Instead of pupils being presented with masses of content to be memorized, they would be faced with a series of problems to solve.

In working out the solutions, however, they would be forced to rely on content and would thus use it in solving their problems. The mastery of content so used would therefore be vastly superior in both efficiency and retention.

SUMMARY

In the previous chapters we have had little difficulty aligning the various views of the learner and the subject matter with the philosophies they represent. Such an alignment is not so easy in dealing with the learning process. The various assumptions about the learning process we have examined in this chapter are often so diverse and so different in their approach to solving the mystery of learning as to make clean, neat alignment impossible.

Too, the divergencies which exist between various philosophies within the same general school of thought make the analysis of them difficult. For instance, connectionism and behaviorism are both associational theories, yet they differ markedly from each other in their interpretation of learning. Thus philosophers of one persuasion may find connectionism fits their school of thought and those of another persuasion may align themselves with behaviorism—yet both may have embraced an associational theory of learning.

Nevertheless, some alignment of these learning theories with theories of the learner and of the subject matter is necessary. We will attempt such an alignment only if you will bear in mind the difficulties and limitations discussed in the preceding paragraphs.

In the previous chapters we have discussed the school of philosophy called Essentialism which views the learner as innately stupid or naive and the truth as something absolute and unchanging. Educators who support the Essentialists' viewpoint vary in their acceptance of learning theory. Some hold tenaciously to faculty psychology despite its being disproved by research. More frequently, however, the Essentialists find support in the associational learning theory. The fact that Essentialists put more emphasis on the subject matter than they do on the learner causes them to seek a learning theory that supports an "outside-to-inside" view. Inasmuch as the associational theory also tends to so view the learning process, these two become mutually supportive.

Genetic psychology unquestionably finds its proper alignment with the Romantic or Idealistic philosophy. The view of man as good by nature and of truth as being of an intuitive nature emphasizes the internal aspects of learning. Genetic psychology's view of learning as a matter of internal development is a natural complement to these views.

Pragmatists have, by and large, found themselves embracing the field theory of learning. The laudatory position given by this theory to problem solving and learning by insight has been eagerly accepted by Pragmatists. However, their view of man as an evolving creature who struggles to find mastery over his environment and of the subject matter as a tool for achieving this goal causes the Pragmatist to reject associational psychology with its view of man as a mere reactor to environment. The field theories are much more in keeping with the dynamic view of life and learning as described by the Pragmatist.

The philosophy we have called Realism is much more difficult to align with a particular theory of learning. The majority of Realistic philosophers tend to favor the field theory. They do so for different reasons than the Pragmatists, however. The common ground in Realism and field theory is the "breadth of learning" idea which is expressed or implied in both. Realism seeks breadth of curriculum because of its view of man as a creature in quest of ultimate truth; field theory sees the environment in the broadest possible terms because this is how the individual perceives it. But not all Realists are eager to accept field theory. Many feel that gestalt psychology needlessly complicates the explanation of learning. Realists tend to see learning as an outside-to-inside affair as do the Associationists. Therefore, some Realists find associational theory more compatible with their view of the learner and of the subject matter.

A natural question which arises from any discussion of learning theory is, "Is it necessary that we accept one of the theories to the exclusion of others?" An eclectic view of learning theory has all of the potentialities and at the same time all of the limitations that such a view has in any philosophic system of thought. It is more likely that the individual will select the one of these approaches which will fit best with his view of the learner and of the subject matter. But he may borrow practices advocated by other theories and be wise in doing so, provided the borrowed practices do not work in opposition to his fundamental assumptions.

Certainly learning is a vast and complicated process and deserves continued examination. We need to continually try to solve the mystery of learning; but it will always remain a miracle.

CHAPTER V

•

THE TEACHING AGENCY

We now turn to the fourth and final of the ingredients that constitute the curriculum—the teaching agency. Thus far we have studied the varying assumptions that we may make as to the nature of the learner, the subject matter, and the process of learning. The fourth element of the curriculum is as important as the first three but is more elusive. This is due in part to its diversity, but it is also because it is difficult to establish cause and effect relationships. In some cases the type of teaching agency we create is the result of our assumptions about the other components of the curriculum; in other cases we adopt certain assumptions about the teaching agency itself and these in turn are reflected in the way in which the teaching agency is selected, organized, and utilized. Thus our assumptions about the teaching agency are at once the cause and the effect of certain curriculum practices.

Viewed in the broadest possible terms, the teaching agency includes virtually all aspects of the environment in which learning occurs. We may use the term *learning environment* to signify this vast panorama of objects and events that compose the learner's world.

As you read this passage you find yourself in an environment in which the thousands of things which compose your surroundings are having their influence upon you. The material printed here is the subject matter of the experience, but the printing itself has been created in such a way as to make it easier for your eye to scan the lines and get meaning from the words. The book itself is an agency of your learning experience, as are—in other situations—pictures, films, and phonograph recordings. All are devices by which subject matter is presented.

Beyond this, the room in which you sit, the temperature, the humidity, etc. are factors which may either distract or encourage your efforts to learn. You also exist in a world of other people who influence your attempts to learn. The very fact that you are motivated to read this book is probably the result of other people, either directly or indirectly, having influenced you to have a desire for intellectual pursuits.

We could go on at great length with this description of the vastness of the learning environment, but of greater value would be an attempt to classify and discuss those factors which have the greatest influence on the curriculum.

If we attempt to classify the various types of learning environments, we find ourselves faced with the fact that any such system of classification is of necessity arbitrary. Let us admit this limitation, however, and examine the teaching agencies in terms that are suited to our purposes here.

The Cultural Milieu. Broadest and most comprehensive of the teaching agencies is the entire culture itself with all of its facets, interrelationships, intricacies, and disparities. This panorama which we may call the cultural milieu represents the totality of folkways, mores, laws, tools, techniques, and institutions which affect our behavior from the day of our birth until we die. To be alive in a culture means that we learn from it and because of it. Even the most ardent non-conformist cannot escape playing the game according to the rules of our society. The culture in which we live also gives us a system of values which motivates us toward desiring certain goals. By our becoming socialized individuals we bring to each learning situation the stamp of our society which in turn is a teaching agency in its broadest terms.

Informal Educational Agencies. In addition to the general culture there are institutions within the society which do not have education as their chief or only aim but which, in an informal—often incidental—way contribute greatly to the education of the individual. These we can call informal agencies because for them education is only a secondary goal.

Typical and most important of these is the family. Although it serves many functions in our society, we cannot ignore the fact that one of its major contributions is to the education of the young. Since the family has the child under its care for such an extended period early in his life, the educational aspects of child rearing by the family cannot be ignored. Indeed, it may be asserted that unless the child gets a good start in his education in the home, little can be done later in the child's life by other agencies to make up for this lack. Other informal agencies would include the church, the immediate community, all levels of government, social and fraternal organizations, the press, labor unions, chambers of commerce—the list could be extended indefinitely—all of which perform an educational function even though this function is secondary to their primary purposes.

Formal Educational Agencies. Our concern in this book, however, is with the one institution which has as its sole purpose the education of our people—the school. Regardless of level, regardless of area of specialization, all schools are dedicated to this one objective. We may label them as formal educational agencies, not because their methods are necessarily formal or conventional, but because they have formally adopted education as their sole aim or purpose.

We have pointed out previously that one cannot avoid learning—that to be alive is to learn. We may well ask, then, what makes the school different from the rest of life? Why do we need formal educational institutions?

A school can do no more than provide an environment in which the student has the maximum opportunity to learn those things which are deemed by the society and by the educators to be of greatest value. Stripped of all side issues, it is the school's only function to provide an environment for learning. In order to accomplish its task of educating the young, it has taken on many incidental tasks and characteristics. It has developed its own administrative structure; it has created auxiliary services such as transportation of pupils and hot lunch programs; and it has provided clubs and social events to meet other needs of its students in order to keep them interested and happy in the school situation.

But at the heart of the school's business is the instructional program, and all these other facets are but incidental to the main task. It behooves us, therefore, to fix our attention on those elements of the school which have the greatest influence on the curriculum and on the instructional program.

As was the case in the other philosophic foundations of the curriculum, there is one central problem which is indicative of all the varying assumptions which can be made about the teaching agency. Put in its simplest terms, the issue is, "What is the proper function of the school in the education of the child?"

We have said that the school has a unique function as the formal educational agency. We have also stated that it provides an environment in which the child has the maximum opportunity to learn those things which society demands that he be taught. But society is not articulate. It is often not even unified in its educational objectives. We must, therefore, find some way of determining the relationship of the school and the society which it serves.

In order for us to get this central problem in more manageable form, it is necessary for us to break it down into several lesser problems. Many such sub-problems could be considered, but for our purposes we shall select three because of their importance to the curriculum and curriculum development.

The first of these problems concerns the relationship of the school to the society as a whole. Throughout history there has been raised again and again the persistent question of whether the school is but the handmaiden of society or whether it has the more dynamic role of leadership. The answer we give to this question will have an influence upon the type of curriculum which the school evolves. But it will also determine such things as the attitude of educators toward community pressure groups and the image which the school presents to its public.

A second issue or subproblem concerns the teacher. Certainly there can be no debate as to the importance of the teacher in the education of a child. Throughout history men have lauded the teacher and his task even though material and status rewards have been slow in coming. There is little question that a society in which there are no people willing to assume the role of the teacher would be doomed to oblivion.

In spite of the recognition of the importance of the teacher, we have been unsuccessful in our efforts to define what makes the master teacher. In the medical profession it is easy to evaluate the worth of a doctor—the more cures he effects, the better doctor he is. But we lack such solid means of evaluation for the effectiveness of teachers. If one hears the statement, "Mr. Brown is a good teacher," what does one infer from it? One may infer anything—from Mr. Brown's being a scholar to such personal characterisics as his having a pleasant voice or a sense of humor. How can the effectiveness of a teacher be ascertained? There are no answers to this question which can be separated from our assumptions about what a teacher should be and what attributes he should possess.

The third of these problems is concerned with the curriculum itself. How should the curriculum be organized or structured in order to provide the maximum opportunity for learning? In the third chapter we discussed the content of the curriculum, but our concern here is for the way in which the curriculum is put together. We must deal with such topics as the order or sequence of learning experiences, the scope or inclusiveness of these experiences, the placement of certain subject matter at certain grade levels, and the division of the curriculum into its various fields or subjects. Inasmuch as most of us are accustomed to a curriculum organized according to subject matter fields and grade levels, we fail to be aware of the many other types of curriculum organization which are possible. The usual or traditional organization is the result of certain assumptions; if we make other assumptions, other forms of structure would serve our purposes better.

Each of these teaching agencies and the issues pertinent to them can be considered in the light of certain assumptions we make about them. The nature, purpose, and type of curriculum which is developed will be the product of these assumptions. Let us therefore examine each of these issues in turn.

THE SCHOOL AND SOCIETY

In order to attack our first major issue let us examine the school as a social institution.

The Teaching Agency

Every society must provide some system whereby the young are taught the ways and values of the culture. This is no less true in primitive societies than in our own. The young boy must learn to hunt, to fight, to gather food, or whatever else is required to sustain his own life and the well-being of the tribe. The young girl must learn the domestic skills pertinent to her role. Through this process primitive societies perpetuate themselves. As societies become more advanced, they also become more complex; however, the processes whereby the child learns to conform to his social roles remain the same.

Not only is it necessary to instruct the child in his role as an adult member of the community, he must also be taught a system of values and the roles of the other members of the society. Most of us have gained this knowledge over so many years and through so gradual a process that we are unaware of our great store of knowledge about our social world and its functions. This process whereby the child learns to conform to his societal role and to become aware of all of the intricacies and varieties of the social order is called *socialization*.

No single characteristic of the present social scene is more outstanding than that of change. Ours is a society in continual revolution; and the greater the rate of change in any culture the greater is the possibility and the need for further change. This "snowballing" or "avalanching" of cultural change produces even greater problems, while the solution to present problems only leads to still greater need for social action in the future.

As an example, the last twenty-five years have seen greater changes in our society than have occurred in the entire past history of Western civilization. The progress in invention and diffusion of knowledge alone is staggering. The harnessing of atomic energy, the probing of outer space, and the progress in medical science—all indicate the vast alterations which have occurred in the last quarter-century. Such revolution is indeed striking, but more prodigious is the realization that the next twenty-five years will produce even greater changes.

This situation—although interesting enough as a subject for purely theoretical study—also produces curricular problems of a real and practical nature. It is because of this social change that the basic question, "Should the school lead or follow society?" has become of such importance. Educators differ tremendously in how they answer this question, and the answers given show not only their personal attitudes but also serve as a key to understanding the kind of educational practices which would result from their views. Answers to this basic question will be varied, but they will fall mainly under four basic approaches.

The Custodial View. Stated in its broadest terms, the custodial view of the school's socialization task is that it should be the guardian of the systems of values which the society has already evolved.

Supporters of this opinion hold that the school's principal task is to *follow* society; that the school should reflect and maintain those social values that have already been established. The educational institution should serve as the guardian of the social system. This is not to deny that the society will change, but in social change education should be an arresting force rather than an encouraging agent. What else, it is argued by those holding the custodial view, can the school do? To predict what the future will hold and to train the child for that future demands a clairvoyance possessed by few, if any, men. How can a school have such mystical powers? We are on much safer ground if we teach children to live in the world as it is and inculcate within them the tried and true values arrived at through centuries of social evolution.

The Creative View. In direct opposition to the view of the school as a retainer of social values is the creative view, which holds that the chief purpose of the school is to assume a role of leadership in bringing about social change. Advocates of the creative view consider social change as not only inevitable, but also desirable. To attempt to retard this change is to stifle and make stagnant the culture. Further, they say, the school has a vital role in forwarding social change. Inasmuch as the ideals and aspirations of the coming generation are shaped by the school, the educational institution can serve as the agent through which progress can be originated. Within the schools children should be taught to create new rules and customs. The entire atmosphere should be one of uninhibited creativity. Ideas of order, discipline, and responsibility should be replaced by ideas of spontaneity and creativity. Through such an educational system, they say, a generation of citizens will come into being who will forward the dynamic quality of life.

The Interactional View. A more "middle-of-the-road" view of the socialization role of the school is found in the interactional view. Supporters of this belief stress the fact that the school and society are part and parcel of each other. Certainly the school takes its cue for direction from the society; but in setting up its program, the school itself becomes a creator of new codes of behavior and social values. Thus the name, interactional view, is descriptive of this persuasion.

The interaction approach is not just a means of escaping the arguments involved in accepting one of the more extreme views. The supporters of the interactional belief maintain that theirs is the only realistic or practical set of assumptions on which a curriculum can be built. It is custodial in that it refuses to cast aside the wisdom gained through centuries of experience of the race; it is creative in that it recognizes that change can and should be brought about through the process of education itself. But most important of all, it accepts the principle of social interaction—that the school neither leads nor follows society, but each reacts to and influences the other.

The Integrative View. Somewhat akin to the interactional view—but still unique—is the integrative view. Supporters of this view are highly impressed with the variety and disparity which is found within our society. In simple, primitive cultures there is a uniformity which makes education simple and direct. Social change is slow; there are few if any debates concerning the system of values to be upheld by the tribe; and the young can be fitted for their lives in their society with a minimum of effort. But as societies become more advanced, they also tend to become more complex and less uniform. Often these elements of the culture become highly diversified and at war with each other. For instance, in our own society the attitudes toward the consumption of alcoholic beverages are highly variable; advertisers seek to promote drinking, but many religious groups preach abstinence. Labor unions argue for what they consider to be the worker's just share of a company's income; the owners maintain that such demands are an encroachment upon their right to a fair profit. These are but samples of the warring factions within our society; on every side the observant person sees evidence of the lack of unity of purpose. Somehow the diversities of our culture must be made understandable to the individual so that he may have the basis on which to build intelligent choices. Those who advocate the integrative view insist that the school has the responsibility for giving the individual the breadth of outlook which will make it possible for him to evaluate his culture and to come to sound decisions about his social world.

Further, they insist that though the school may encourage creativity, the means of building it are not through unrestrained or uninhibited activity. True creativity—creativity with social value—comes through the assumption of responsibility and discipline. If one is to change existing cultural patterns, he must first have a thorough grounding in the culture as it is. Put another way, one must first be schooled in the rules of society before he can learn to break these rules wisely.

THE SOCIALIZATION TASK AND THE CURRICULUM

These four concepts of the socialization task of the school are likely to seem nebulous and impractical unless we can discover a way to relate them to the realities of teaching and the curriculum. Let us look at some examples of curriculum practices growing out of the adoption of these various views.

The field of social studies offers many excellent examples from which we may draw these comparisons. A good topic for purposes of illustration is that of race relations. If we were to adopt a custodial view in teaching this topic, we would emphasize how we have been able to work out our problems in the past without resorting to demonstrations, court decisions, or new laws. Students would be taught the value of a stable society founded on the principle of separation of the races. The acceptance of a creative view, on the other hand, would lead to a rejection of all past behavior patterns that have existed in race relations. Each child would be encouraged to reach his own conclusions about the subject, but above all, the child would be protected from and encouraged to cast off all prejudices of his elders. The interactional view would advocate the thorough study of race relations as a contemporary problem in the lives of the students. High sounding generalities would be discarded, for in the long run race relations must become personal relations. According to this view, children must be guided toward the critical examination of their own relations with members of other races as a means of achieving better race relations in society as a whole. Finally, the supporters of the integrative view would approach the topic by way of a thorough study of the history and contemporary state of the problem. Varying opinions and ideas would be studied in order to get a sound background on which the opinion of the student could be formed.

Another example can be found in the field of art, where the variations in viewpoint have been outstandingly evident for a number of years. Those who support the custodial view of the art curriculum state that the child must be taught the principles of design, the way to use materials, the techniques of drawing, painting, etc. The child who is most able to master these basic skills can be regarded as the best artist, while the child who cannot master them will never be able to express himself through the medium of art. An art teacher who advocates the creative view, however, would have none of such teaching; instead he would turn the children loose and by encouragement and motivation would help them express themselves through whatever materials and in whatever way they wish. The ultimate aim of such teaching would be the free, uninhibited expression of the child's aesthetic feelings and emotions. The interactionists would insist that the teaching of techniques and use of materials should be the outgrowth of the problem of creativity which the pupil is facing. The child should be encouraged to express some idea or feeling but should then be aided and guided toward the skills and materials which would produce the best expression of them. The supporters of the integrative view would begin as do those who hold the custodial view. The child should be taught the basics or fundamentals of design, techniques, and the use of materials. The discipline of the art must precede the creative activity in the art. However when he has mastered this discipline, they would go on to say, he should be encouraged to deviate from them as suits his purposes. This is not to say that creativity is to be stifled until the basics or fundamentals are mastered; but the child must learn that there are certain techniques which produce certain results. If he is to succeed in communicating his feelings, he must capitalize on what earlier men have found to be effective. When he has learned these fundamentals, he may progress to create other techniques, design forms, and structures by which he can express himself more effectively.

Still other examples of the variations in these four views can be found in the teaching of language arts. Let us look at the teaching of English usage as it reflects the views we have discussed. Those who advocate the custodial approach would teach the student to speak and write according to the established rules of grammar, usage, and diction. No deviation from these rules would be allowed inasmuch as they have been established by generations of the best writers and speakers. If students were allowed to deviate from this established usage, the result would be a total breakdown of the language, with communication becoming impossible. If, however, the teacher adopts the creative approach in teaching usage, he will dispense with the rule book. The sole criterion for usage will be communication. If the child says, "I ain't got no book," he is perfectly clear in his communication and should not be corrected. So long as our words express our thoughts meaningfully and clearly, language has served its purpose. Interactionists, on the other hand, stress the changing nature of the language. Certain forms are preferable only because better speakers and writers have established them as desirable. Further, language propriety varies according to the situation, the listeners, and the level of usage. Children should not be taught that certain forms are "right" and others "wrong." They must be taught how to adapt their language to the demands of the situation. Some forms should be taught as preferable, but the stilted, overly-correct usage is discouraged as well. Finally, the integrational view would hold that the student must first learn the rules of established usage and then be guided to see how these rules may be varied so as to create more effective use of the language. One cannot vary unless he has something positive to vary from. Principles of sound language usage must be mastered first, but then the individual can go on to develop his own unique patterns of usage.

THE TEACHER

Probably no single factor in education has been more open to discussion in recent years than the teacher. Most of the arguments have concerned the nature of teacher preparation in our colleges and universities, but the implications involve far more than teacher education programs. Also involved are such things as the selection of people to enter the profession, the type of experiences which best prepare them to teach, the type of professional organizations to which they should belong, the protections to be afforded them through such devices as tenure and retirement policies, the opportunities and responsibilities implied in the practice of their profession, and the matter of their academic freedom.

It is no wonder, therefore, that there are many different opinions as to the teacher and his role, and these opinions are crucial in understanding the relationship of the teacher to the curriculum.

Probably the most widely accepted view of the teacher is that of the scholar and imparter of knowledge. It is maintained that the teacher's primary task is to be a master of his discipline in order that he may share this knowledge with his students. It is assumed that if the teacher has a thorough knowledge of his subjects, he will have no difficulty in imparting this knowledge, and, since this is the aim of education, there is nothing more to be desired in the teacher. From this point of view, the professional preparation of such a teacher should be within the fields in which he will teach, and his professional affiliations should be with scholars who share the responsibility of teaching in these fields.

However, the increasing emphasis given to the child as the principal concern in education which developed in the United States in the late nineteenth and early twentieth centuries brought forth new concepts of the teacher and his role.

The postulate was developed among some educators that the successful teacher is the one who has the greatest possible insight into children's behavior and personalities. Such a teacher is one who is highly perceptive of the needs of the children and the way in which these needs can be met. He should be able to observe the behavior of children, to analyze it, and to relate to them in as positive a fashion as possible. The teacher's preparation should emphasize these attributes with training in psychology and child study. According to them, more than any other characteristic to be developed in the prospective teacher would be the traits of understanding of, appreciation for, and empathy with the children he will teach.

Other educational writers and thinkers developed a concept of the teacher as a guide and organizer of learning experiences. This doctrine puts its emphasis on the learning process and its direction rather than on either the content or the child. It would hold that although the knowledge of content is of importance to the teacher, it is the teacher's ability to create situations which provide maximum opportunity for learning that is his most desirable attribute. The teacher must be able to plan the experiences so as to create problems which students will find challenging and interesting. Teacher preparations should, therefore, emphasize methods of instruction, but not just how to present information. Emphasis should be given to the methods of problem solving and the development of the attributes of rational thinking and intellectual integrity.

Still others began to view the teacher from the point of view of the kind of person he is rather than what he knows or the methods he uses. It was argued by them that students identify with the teacher and will emulate his traits. It is, therefore, vital that the teacher reflect characteristics which are worthy of this emulation. Although they admitted that an exact listing of these traits is impossible, supporters of this view did attempt to develop the main headings under which such traits would be listed. Above all else, the teacher should be characterized by a breadth of wisdom and understanding. As opposed to the view of the teacher as merely being knowledgeable in his own subject, they saw the ideal teacher as having extended knowledge over many fields. The English teacher should know something of music, art, history, agriculture — every field of human endeavor. This knowledge should be required of every teacher on the school staff. Only if the teacher is broadly educated in many fields can he see his own field in the perspective that makes for true mastery. He should also possess the trait of enthusiasm, and have the ability to share his experiences and knowledge with his students. He should be skilled in methods of organizing and presenting information so as to insure the maximum learning of his pupils; he should be devoted to learning; and he should be the example of the individual who seeks to know more and more about his world. He should possess an inquiring mind and an insatiable appetite for learning. Such a teacher seems an impossible ideal of a person, but to the supporters of this conviction the teacher is of paramount importance and can only be described in idealistic terms.

CURRICULUM ORGANIZATION

As the title of this book indicates, our chief concern is the curriculum. Our philosophy will determine not only its content but also its organization or structure. Just as the assumptions we have made about the ingredients of the curriculum have been shown to shape curriculum practices, so here too the assumptions we make determine how the curriculum will be organized.

Three dominant types of curriculum organization have been evolved and each deserves our examination.

The Separate Subjects Curriculum. The oldest, most widely used, and best known type of curriculum organization is the separate subjects curriculum. It is this structure that is found in most schools of our country. Each subject is taught as a separate entity. In the elementary school there is a daily reading period, a spelling lesson, a social studies period, etc. In the high school the demarcations are even more clear with different classrooms and different teachers separating the subjects; any relationships which might exist between two or more subjects are left unnoticed by teachers who zealously guard their own courses and disdain to recognize others. As the term *separate subjects* indicates, the various experiences which constitute the pupil's school life are organized around a compartmentalized subject content.

The separate subjects curriculum has led to the acceptance of subject matter mastery as the main goal to be achieved. This has caused great emphasis to be given to such learning tasks as definition, classification, and memorization. Other tasks, such as application, analysis, and problem solving have been largely neglected.

The observer of the separate subjects curriculum in action is immediately impressed by the fact that the students are expected to master certain facts and concepts without question. The subject matter content becomes an authority to which all students must subscribe.

Several major strengths may be cited for a curriculum so designed. Among the more outstanding is that it provides maximum security for both teacher and student. Under such a curriculum plan the teacher knows what is expected of him. He is to "cover the book," or some other definite assignment. Likewise, the student knows what is expected of him and where he stands. He knows that if he learns a certain percentage of the information included, he will "pass." This provides him with a constant source of security.

Too, the separate subjects curriculum assures a logical framework for the organization of learning experiences. Chronological order of historical events and the use of cause-and-effect principles in science are examples of how this curriculum structure assures order and consistency in learning experiences which might otherwise be orderless.

Finally, it makes for easy evaluation. Inasmuch as the emphasis is on subject matter mastery, achievement testing is the only type of evaluation needed. Other products of schooling, such as habits and attitudes—products which are more difficult to evaluate—are not so important in the separate subjects curriculum.

One of the major weaknesses of this curriculum organization, however, is its failure to make the students aware of the relationships between the various areas of human knowledge. One of the most valuable attributes an education can give to an individual is the awareness of these relationships and interrelationships. The separate subjects curriculum makes no provision for helping the student see the more subtle or even the more obvious of these relationships. It is no wonder that teachers in schools where the separate subjects curriculum is used are often disturbed that students are unable to use the mathematics they have learned when they come into the science class, or that students fail to see the relationship between the study of American history and the study of the literature of our nation.

The desire to overcome this weakness has led to a variation in this type of curriculum organization called *correlation*. Many different plans for correlation have been used, but all attempt to achieve the same purpose—that of helping the student to become aware of the relationships between subject areas studied.

For instance, in the *broad fields program* the courses are no longer retained as separate subjects but are fused for teaching purposes. Class periods are combined so that a single teacher teaches as one unified course that which was formerly taught in two or more separate courses. Thus, the broad fields curriculum might offer a course in social studies which includes material which was formerly taught in history, geography, political science, and any other subject in the social science area. Likewise, American history and American literature might be combined into a single, unified course. However, one weakness of the broad fields curriculum is that one of the subjects so combined usually suffers in the process. Teachers of broad fields subjects generally have a preference for one of the subjects so that it becomes the principal one and others become mere attachments.

At the present time the separate subjects curriculum or some modification thereof, such as the board fields program, seems destined to remain the dominant type of curriculum organization in our schools. There is good reason for its popularity. The continued increase in the store of human knowledge has caused specialization to become more and more necessary. Therefore a situation exists which is advantageous to the continuation of the separate subjects curriculum.

The Child-Centered Curriculum. As we have pointed out, the separate subjects curriculum is so prevalent that one may be led to the conclusion that it is the only possible way to organize the curriculum. But other alternatives are possible, and one of the more outstanding of these is the child-centered curriculum which is organized around the felt needs of the pupils. Traditional subject matter lines are abolished under the child-centered curriculum inasmuch as content mastery is no longer the goal to be sought. Instead, the content of the curriculum is determined by what the pupils themselves feel to be of value to them. The emphasis in such a curriculum plan is placed upon creative activity. Such an organization of the curriculum would be characterized by pupils busy with all types of activity aimed at bringing from each individual the best that is within him—the realization of his own potentialities. In this plan students would make mistakes, but they would learn through trial and error; and according to those who advocate such a plan, this learning would have the advantage of being through natural consequences rather than the result of imposed authority.

The child-centered curriculum has one great strength which no other curriculum plan can equal. This strength is the ability to capture and to utilize the interest of students. When interest is high, learning is high. This we know from research, and no other curriculum structure so catches the fascination of the child as this one.

But there are also certain major weaknesses in this child-centered curriculum. One of the more outstanding of these is its lack of security. Since no goals are predetermined, since there is no definite information content in the course of study, neither student nor teacher knows where he stands. Such uncertainty is bound to result in insecurity for all concerned. It is also to be noted that the highly individual character of the child-centered curriculum makes the achievement of any social goals impossible. So long as children of any age are allowed to follow their own whims, it is doubtful that they will learn to respect the rights of others or to cooperate toward the achievement of a group goal.

The Experience-Centered Curriculum. Another of these curriculum organization patterns is the experience-centered curriculum which puts its emphasis on the individual student's experiences, his seeking to find solutions to his own problems of living, his discovery of concepts and generalizations, and his becoming aware of his unique role in a complex society. In the experience-centered curriculum the individual's experience is the starting point of all curriculum planning and action. This curriculum structure is marked by an absence of traditional subject matter lines, since the subject matter content is determined by the need of the individual rather than being predetermined by expert opinion of what the child should know.

Emphases in the experience-centered curriculum are given to such traits and competencies as problem solving, analysis, and attitudes. It is with these as tools that the citizens of today's society control and utilize their experiences. In such a curriculum organization subject matter is not ignored, however, as it is in the child-centered curriculum. Instead, the subject matter to be used is determined by the problems the student must face. The learning experiences which the pupils live through are not left to chance or to the whim or felt needs of the pupils. They are the result of the cooperative planning of all concerned by which learning objectives are carefully defined. These objectives are not statements of individual desires; they are built on the needs of the individual and the society. The school program in the experience-centered curriculum is one in which the day-to-day activities which are built around problematic experiences of students, are planned and carried through by the joint action of teachers, students, community, and all other interested groups.

Among the more outstanding strengths of the experience-centered curriculum is the fact that it is geared to the needs and interests of the pupils. The solution of real problems through first hand experience guarantees learning that is lasting and vital. It is also in keeping with the principle of continually moving the student from his present state of knowledge to that which is more advanced and more difficult.

There is one limitation to the experience-centered approach. This is that it gives no assurance that the cultural heritage will be learned. Unless some particular item of subject matter is needed to solve some student's problem, it will not find its way into the curriculum. It is conceivable that a student might get through twelve years of schooling without the most rudimentary knowledge of American history or English literature, simply because he has never been presented with a problem that demands this subject matter to aid in the solution.

The advocates of the experience-centered curriculum are second in number only to those who support the separate subjects curriculum. The chief competition of the future seems destined to be between these two. Even if the experience-centered curriculum should prove to be the more successful, however, it will still require a long hard struggle to replace the separate subjects curriculum. Meanwhile, even though the separate subjects curriculum seems deeply entrenched, other forms of curriculum organization have made definite contributions to traditional curriculum patterns so that the present day curriculum in most schools is a combination of several or all types of curriculum structure.

In the early chapters of this text we have shown that most philosophies of the curriculum can be classified as belonging to four major schools of thought: Essentialism, Idealism, Pragmatism, and Realism. Each of these philosophies has its unique view of the learner, the subject matter, and the learning process. In like manner their beliefs about the teaching agency can be aligned with these philosophies.

Essentialism by its very nature would tend to support the custodial view of the relationship of school and society. His doctrine of conformity because of man's naive nature, his view of the truth as being absolute and unchanging, and his concept of learning for mental discipline or as an atomistic process would cause the Essentialist to look with disdain on the learning which is divorced from the conventional wisdom of our society. In like manner, the teacher would be viewed as a scholar and as a master of his subject; teacher characteristics such as methods of teaching and understanding of children would be regarded as unimportant or secondary to the major tasks and responsibilities of the teacher. Essentialists also tend to support the separate subjects curriculum. The authoritarian orientation of this type of curriculum organization fits logically with the other assumptions of Essentialism.

The philosophy which we have labeled as Idealism is a

"natural" to support the creative view of the relationship of school and society. If we view the child as being innately good and the society as a threat to his freedom it would then follow that the chief task of the school is to continually evaluate the society and to advocate changes which would bring into being a world in which each individual has the opportunity to develop his natural potentialities to the fullest. The teacher's main task should evolve from his understanding of and his ability to relate to his students. Idealists would support the child-centered curriculum, for the belief in the child as the ultimate source of all good makes the child-centered curriculum a logical outcome of such an assumption.

Pragmatists tend to support the interactional view of the school's role as a social institution. Dissatisfied with education for the status quo and yet practical enough to realize the school must educate children to live in a society with all of its rules and regulations, Pragmatists advocate this interactional view. To the Pragmatist the teacher should be a guide or organizer of curriculum experiences. The ability to define problems and to create an environment which stimulates the child to solve these problems—in short, method—is the greatest asset a teacher can possess. The experience-centered curriculum is a logical corollary to the other assumptions of the Pragmatists, for the emphasis on solving problems which are real and meaningful to the learner is the common element of all curricular objectives advocated by the Pragmatic philosophy.

It is the Realist who sees the curriculum as an agency which can and should help the child develop sound relevant judgments about the many divergent movements and opinions which exist within his social world. The Realist's continual concern about the breadth of knowledge causes him to come head-on with the variations and divergencies of our culture, and he seeks to bring these together in some integrated view. He therefore supports the integrative view of the relation of school and society. To the Realist the teacher must be a person worthy of his students' emulation. He should be a scholar of all parts of his world, he should be capable of dispensing this information, and above all else he should be devoted to learning as the ultimate aim of education and of life. The Realist finds it more difficult, however, to endorse or align himself with a particular type of curriculum organization. His concern for learning causes him to lean toward the separate subjects curriculum, but he objects to the specialization implied in such a curriculum structure. He therefore usually advocates some modification of the separate subjects curriculum—such as the broad fields program—which gives the student the breadth of knowledge which the Realist thinks is so desirable.

The four philosophies we have studied have as varied a view of the teaching agency as they had of the learner, the thing learned, and the learning process. The totality of these views is reflected in the varying aims, methods, content, and organization of the curriculum.

CHAPTER VI

•

THE WAY FORWARD

This book was written for only one purpose—to lead the reader
to an examination of his own assumptions about the nature
and purpose of the curriculum. In our first chapter we showed
the importance of a person's having guides to action which
have the attributes of reliability, validity, and consistency. It
is the author's contention that far too few educators have gone
through the agonizing business of examining their own views
in the cold light of philosophy. We are likely to make statements about the curriculum, its evaluation, and its development
which are merely the results of reaction to immediate situations, or to hold tenaciously to past practices without examining either the bases or the ultimate results of our efforts. The
consequences of this lack of philosophic investigation are curriculums which are often divergent, confused, and indefensible
to either the educational world or the lay public. If this book
has helped you bring order to your own thinking about the
curriculum and its philosophic bases it has accomplished its task.

It has not been the claim of this book to present an ex-
haustive or comprehensive treatment of education philosophy.
We have presented only four major schools of philosophic
thought—Essentialism, Idealism, Pragmatism, and Realism.
True, we have examined many subfields of these four, but we
have left unmentioned many other views which have a potential to influence the curriculum. Our basis for the selection of
these four has been that in the present educational scene they
are characteristic of most of the views held toward the curriculum. Nor have we traced the implications of these philosophies for other parts of our educational efforts; such areas

as educational administration and auxiliary services have only been mentioned in passing, if at all. If the reader's interests take him in these directions, he can use the same methods of analysis in these areas that we have suggested for the curriculum.

Our presentation of these four philosophic positions has pivoted about the four major areas of concern in curriculum development—the learner, the subject matter, the learning process, and the teaching agency. As we have seen, there is a "fitting together" within each of the philosophies of its view of each of these components. For example, the Essentialists' view of the child as a naive and unwilling participant in learning fits easily with the correspondence theory of truth, with faculty psychology or the associational learning theory, and with the custodial view of the teaching agency. This correlation of views has been discussed in the summary for each chapter; however, it is wise to recapitulate here. The table presented here can help you see these interrelationships.

It was not our aim to present an exposition of a particular philosophic position. We did not attempt to convince the reader of the superiority of any doctrine. Nevertheless, the author must admit to holding one of the views here discussed. Like most students of the subject, he has done no small amount of soul searching to find a set of assumptions which he could accept emotionally as well as intellectually. The result has been his adoption of the Realistic philosophy. It possesses those characteristics of consistency, intellectual reasonableness, and emotional palatability which he can readily accept. Nevertheless, he has attempted to avoid making this view more attractive to the reader than the others. In attempting such writing there is always the danger of "leaning over backwards" so that the net effect is to make the author's own belief less appealing than the others.

PHILOSOPHY AND CURRICULUM TODAY

As one views the educational scene today one is impressed with the confusion in the purpose and direction of the efforts being made. Rarely before in the history of education has there been less consistency or unity in the curriculums of our schools. Several factors have brought about this state of affairs.

110

Table I

	View of the Child	View of the Subject Matter	View of the Learning Process	View of the Teaching Agency
ESSENTIALISM	Theory of Natural Evil: The child a fugitive from learning.	Correspondence Theory of Truth: Subject matter the prime concern in curriculum development.	Faculty Psychology or Associational Theory: Learning through drill on particulars.	Custodial View of School and Society: Teacher as Master Scholar. Separate Subjects Curriculum.
IDEALISM	Theory of Natural Good: The child a developing organism who is aware of his own needs.	Intuitive Theory of Truth: Child's felt needs the starting point in curriculum development.	Genetic Psychology: Learning and development are synonymous.	Creative View of School and Society: Teacher as a Friend and Guide. Child-Centered Curriculum.
PRAGMATISM	Theory of Evolving Man: The child an organism struggling to achieve adjustment.	Pragmatic Theory of Truth: Content must be the result of what is needed to solve problems.	Field Theory: Emphasis on problem solving.	Interactional View of School and Society: Teacher as the Organizer of Learning Experiences. Experience-Centered Curriculum.
REALISM	Theory of Aspiring Man: The child a seeker of wisdom with a natural appetite for learning.	Coherence Theory of Truth: Content is as vast as the universe— all knowledge is worthy of inclusion in the curriculum.	Field Theory: Emphasis on seeing relationships which exist between fields of knowledge.	Integrative View of School and Society: Teacher as a Learning Scholar. Separate Subjects Curriculum with modification to provide for inter-relationships.

The first is the vast number of curriculum changes. The advancements in educational technology of the last decade have produced changes which continually challenge us. Among other innovations we have seen the widespread use of instructional television, the utilization of programmed learning, and the vast increase in funds from the federal government for the improvement of school programs and for research. Instead of these innovations being gradually integrated into existing curriculum patterns on the basis of a unified philosophy, they have often swiftly dominated the curriculum, and they have been closely examined only after they have become an entrenched part of the school program. Few schools can be found that are truly in command of their curriculum changes; instead curriculum changes have been forced upon them.

Second, the great number of curriculum changes is matched by a corresponding diffusion in philosophy itself. In a larger context, modern man finds himself with few philosophic positions which are in any sense fixed or universal in acceptance. Old systems of values are fading, and new ones have not been created to fill the void. In the philosophy of the curriculum this same lack of stability is evident. Teachers, supervisors, and curriculum directors are searching desperately for answers; they are rewarded not with solutions, but with more and greater questions and problems.

Finally, there is a dearth of new and significant philosophy which is applicable to the curriculum. Progress in educational thought is not a slow, regular growth; it moves by fits and starts. Periodically some individual or group comes forth with a new way of looking at things which changes our thinking radically, causes us to gain new insights and new directions, and to try to bring some order out of the chaos and give unity to our thoughts and efforts. As we are busy with our day-to-day efforts of planning, teaching, and evaluating, someone may suddenly publish a book or formulate a new doctrine—and things are never the same again. From these periodic innovations new strength may emerge, and we may find ourselves broadening our outlook and engaging in new and different practices which get their meaning from the new doctrines. Locke brought about such innovations in the seventeenth century; Rousseau in the eighteenth; Spencer in the nineteenth; and Dewey early in the twentieth. But since then no such prophet has emerged; no new doctrine has emerged to take the educational world by storm. Instead we find ourselves in a state of ferment with no school of thought taking unchallenged leadership. Conservatives would have us return to the curriculum patterns of the past; Existentialists would have us give the individual the position of prominence; others attempt to reexamine the doctrines of Dewey to discover new values within them. But all of these are reflections of the past, no new set of doctrines has been created to give us the vigorous leadership we need. The time is ripe for such a philosophy to be formulated but of course only time will tell if such a new philosophy will emerge.

In another sense, however, the present period is marked by occurrences and outlooks which make it a fertile time for the growth of philosophy. Among the more striking characteristics of the new era has been its emphasis on educational research. The development of computers and computer mathematics has made possible a level of statistical back-up for research which would have been impossible a decade ago. Furthermore, the activities of the federal government in funding research projects as well as the support of private foundations have heightened interests and efforts in research.

Noteworthy, too, is the fact that graduate schools of education are producing scholars who are well trained in research outlook and skills. A new breed has emerged which has the capacity to bring about significant curricular change through research. The excitement of the present period augurs well for the emergence of a philosophy to match the vitality and the dynamic attributes of contemporary research.

Philosophy, Curriculum, and the Student

The present circumstances emphasize the need for the educator to work long and hard in the examination of his own assumptions as to the nature and purposes of the curriculum. Without a new spokesman in the field of educational philosophy it becomes doubly important for each individual to become his own spokesman, to examine his own assumptions, and to create his own philosophy on which a curriculum can be based. And even if a prophet were to emerge, it would be necessary that each educator evaluate the new spokesman. Early in this book we showed the disadvantages of following the crowd in our educational endeavors. If we are to evaluate the multitude of claims made for our allegiance, we must have sound criteria with which to judge them. The need for the development of our personal philosophy is, therefore, as much needed in this case as if there were no innovations to demand our acceptance or rejection.

If we are to meet this challenge, we must continue to examine, to criticize, and to evaluate our assumptions and the curriculum patterns which result from them. There are at least two avenues which are open to us in such a continuing appraisal.

The first is by study of the curriculum itself. For active teachers or curriculum workers engaged in day-to-day, on-the-job decision making, long hours of philosophic reflection are a luxury that few can afford. This does not mean that continuing examination of philosophy is impossible. It does mean that as we work on new curriculum practices, we should work within a context of philosophy. Rather than accepting or rejecting curriculum changes on the basis of momentary pressures or emotional reaction, we should try to use our philosophy as a guide. Rather than initiating curriculum development merely because it seems the thing to do at the moment, it should be initiated in a deliberate attempt to find curriculum practices which more accurately reflect our system of values and the goals which we seek.

For others who have the time, the continual study of philosophy can prove a rewarding experience. Should you be so fortunate, and so inclined, this study is one which has unlimited possibilities and challenges. We have already seen what a vast and fascinating field philosophy is. You should not restrict yourself to the study of educational philosophy; virtually every field of philosophy can prove a rewarding adventure. No field is without its implications for the curriculum. It is hoped that if this book has done nothing else, it has whetted your appetite for a further study of philosophy. Perhaps it has given you some idea of what it means to think philosophically. Perhaps it has produced in you that impact which competent readers find when first being confronted with philosophic thought—namely, the new outlook as well as the uncertainty and insecurity which accompany such an outlook. Should this uncertainty seem undesirable, let us hasten to say it is both valuable and temporary. It represents a stage of intellectual emancipation through which every philosopher has passed. Only by first experiencing this doubt and uncertainty can we become engaged in higher levels of concept formation.

Philosophic thought to the educator must be more than intellectual gymnastics; it must result in changes in school practices. The basic thesis of this book is that the assumptions one makes about the various ingredients or components of the curriculum do make a great difference in the type of curriculum he advocates. It remains for the educator to determine whether the philosophy he gives lip service to becomes a real force in shaping the curriculum over which he exerts influence.

Philosophy is, in the long run, an individual matter. School staffs and committees may meet and make declarations of purposes or of school policy, but it is in each individual's own thinking that philosophy is born and developed. Each of us must examine and reexamine his beliefs and attitudes; add to and discard from his compilation of ideas; emotionally accept and reject new doctrines; and from the hard stuff of his own thought and experience build his philosophy. Such a course is at once a challenge and an opportunity, and each of us must decide for himself whether he will meet or avoid this challenge and opportunity.

A BIBLIOGRAPHY FOR FURTHER
READING

•

The readings listed here are not intended to be a complete or comprehensive bibliography of the subjects treated. The books and articles have been selected so as to present a variety of views. It is hoped that the better student will use them as a springboard to still further inquiry.

Chapter I: Introduction

Brackenbury, Robert L. *Getting Down to Cases*. New York: Putnams, 1959.

Broudy, Harry S. *Building a Philosophy of Education*. Englewood Cliffs, New Jersey: Prentice-Hall, 1961. Chapter I.

Brubacher, John S. "The Challenge to Philosophize about Education," in *Modern Philosophies and Education*, 54th Yearbook, NSSE, Part I; 1955.

Brubacher, John S. *Eclectic Philosophy of Education*. Englewood Cliffs, New Jersey: Prentice-Hall, 1962, Chapter I.

Ducasse, C. J. "What Can Philosophy Contribute to Educational Theory?" *Harvard Educational Review*, Fall, 1958.

Phenix, Phillip H. *Philosophy of Education*. New York: Holt, Rinehart, and Winston, 1958. Chapter I.

Price, Kingsley. *Education and Philosophic Thought*. Boston: Allyn and Bacon, 1962. Chapter I.

Reid, Louis A. *Philosophy and Education*. New York: Random House, 1962. Chapters I and II.

Scheffler, Israel. *Philosophy and Education*. Boston: Allyn and Bacon, 1958. Introduction.

Weber, Christian O. *Basic Philosophies of Education*. New York: Rinehart, 1960. Chapter I.

A Bibliography for Further Reading

Chapter II: The Learner

Ausubel, David P. "Viewpoints from Related Disciplines: Human Growth and Development," *Teachers College Record,* February, 1959.

Brauner, Charles J. *American Educational Theory.* Englewood Cliffs, New Jersey: Prentice-Hall, 1964. Chapter V.

Broudy, Harry S. *Building a Philosophy of Education.* Englewood Cliffs, New Jersey: Prentice-Hall, 1961. Chapter III.

Brubacher, John S. *Eclectic Philosophy of Education.* Englewood Cliffs, New Jersey: Prentice-Hall, 1962. Chapter III.

Childs, John L. *Education and the Philosophy of Experimentalism.* New York: Appleton-Century, 1931. Chapter IV.

Douglass, Harl R. *The High School Curriculum.* New York: Ronald, 1964. Chapter III.

Montagu, Ashley. "Our Changing Conception of Human Nature," *Impact of Science on Society,* Winter, 1952.

Morris, Van Cleve. "Existentialism and Education," *Educational Theory,* October, 1954.

Phenix, Philip H. *Philosophy of Education.* New York: Holt, Rinehart and Winston, 1958. Chapters XXV and XXVI.

Price, Kingsley. *Education and Philosophic Thought.* Boston: Allyn and Bacon, 1962. Chapter VII.

Shuster, Albert H. and Proghoft, Milton E. *The Emerging Elementary Curriculum.* Columbus, Ohio: Merrill, 1963. Chapter II.

Soderquist, Harold O. *The Person and Education.* Columbus, Ohio: Merrill, 1964. Chapter VI.

Wynne, John P. *Theories of Education.* New York: Harper and Row, 1963. Chapters II, V, and VI.

Chapter III: The Subject Matter

Bagley, William C. "The Significance of the Essentialist Movement in Educational Theory," *Classical Journal,* March, 1939.

Brubacher, John S. *Eclectic Philosophy of Education.* Englewood Cliffs, New Jersey: Prentice-Hall, 1962. Chapter II.

Clark, Leonard H. *The American Secondary School Curriculum.* New York: Macmillan, 1965. Chapter II.

Dewey, John. "The Challenge to Liberal Thought," *Fortune,* August, 1944.

Hook, Sidney. "Modern Education and Its Critics," *Seventh Yearbook; Association of Colleges for Teacher Education.* 1954.

Lee, Gordon C. *Education and Democratic Ideals.* New York: Harcourt, Brace, and World, 1965.

National Society for the Study of Education. *Philosophies of Education.* 41st Yearbook, Part I, 1942. Chapters II, III, IV, and V.

Parker, J. Cecil *et al. Curriculum in America.* New York: Crowell, 1962. Chapter II.

Phenix, Philip H. *Philosophy of Education.* New York: Holt, Rinehart, and Winston, 1958. Chapters XVII and XXVIII.

Price, Kingsley. *Education and Philosophic Thought.* Boston: Allyn and Bacon, 1962. Chapter X.

Reid, Louis A. *Philosophy and Education.* New York: Random House, 1962. Chapters XI and XII.

Weber, Christian O. *Basic Philosophies of Education.* New York: Rinehart, 1960. Chapters XIV, XV, and XVI.

Weisberg, Harold. "Tradition and the Traditionalists," in Scheffler, Israel. *Philosophy and Education.* Boston: Allyn and Bacon, 1958.

Wynne, John P. *Theories of Education.* New York: Harper and Row, 1963. Chapters V, X, and XII.

Chapter IV: The Learning Process

Bigge, Morris L. "Theories of Learning," *NEA Journal,* March, 1966.

Brubacher, John S. *Eclectic Philosophy of Education.* Englewood Cliffs, New Jersey: Prentice-Hall, 1962. Chapter IV.

Craig, Robert C. *The Psychology of Learning in the Classroom.* New York: Macmillan, 1966.

Kramer, Samuel A. "Are Theories of Learning Helpful?" *Educational Forum,* January, 1955.

Mursell, James L. "The Miracle of Learning," *Atlantic,* June, 1935.

Price, Kingsley. *Education and Philosophic Thought.* Boston: Allyn and Bacon, 1962. Chapter VI.

Spence, Kenneth W. "The Relation of Learning Theory to the Technology of Education," *Harvard Educational Review,* Spring, 1959.

Taba, Hilda. *Curriculum Development.* New York: Harcourt, Brace and World, 1962. Chapter VI.

Travers, John F. *Learning: Analysis and Applications.* New York: David McKay, 1965. Chapter VIII.

Watson, Goodwin. "What Do We Know About Learning?" *NEA Journal,* March, 1963.

Weber, Christian O. *Basic Philosophies of Education.* New York: Rinehart, 1960. Chapter VI.

Wynne, John P. *Theories of Education.* New York: Harper and Row, 1963. Chapters I and IV.

Chapter V: The Teaching Agency

Broudy, Harry S. *Building a Philosophy of Education.* Englewood Cliffs, New Jersey: Prentice-Hall, 1961. Chapters IV, XII, XIII, and XIV.

Brubacher, John S. *Eclectic Philosophy of Education.* Englewood Cliffs, New Jersey: Prentice-Hall, 1962. Chapters XV, XVI, and XXIII.

Clark, Leonard H. *The American Secondary School Curriculum.* New York: Macmillan, 1965. Chapters IV and VII.

Douglass, Harl R. *The High School Curriculum.* New York: Ronald, 1964. Chapters IV and V.

Geiger, George R. "An Experimentalist Approach to Education," in *Modern Philosophies and Education.* 54th Yearbook, NSSE, Part I: 1955.

Getzels, Jacob W. "Changing Values Challenge the Schools," *School Review,* March, 1957.

Phenix, Philip H. *Philosophy of Education.* New York: Holt, Rinehart and Winston, 1958. Chapters IV and IX.

Reid, Louis A. *Philosophy and Education.* New York: Random House, 1962. Chapters VI and X.

Russell, Bertrand. "The Function of a Teacher," *Harpers,* June, 1940.

Taba, Hilda. *Curriculum Development.* New York: Harcourt, Brace and World, 1962. Chapters II, XVIII, and XXI.

Weber, Christian O. *Basic Philosophies of Education.* New York: Rinehart, 1960. Chapter XVII.

Wilde, John. "Education and Human Society: A Realistic View," in *Modern Philosophies and Education.* 54th Yearbook, NSSE, Part I; 1955.

Williams, Lloyd P. "Some Criticisms of American Life and Education," *Educational Forum,* May, 1959.

          Printed in U.S.A.